Stanislaus Henkels

Extraordinary collection of Washington's letters

Washington relics, revolutionary documents

Stanislaus Henkels

Extraordinary collection of Washington's letters
Washington relics, revolutionary documents

ISBN/EAN: 9783337231859

Printed in Europe, USA, Canada, Australia, Japan

Cover: Foto ©ninafisch / pixelio.de

More available books at **www.hansebooks.com**

CATALOGUE No. 677

An
Extraordinary Collection
of
Washington's Letters
Washington Relics
Revolutionary Documents

and

The Rarest Works on American
History

also

Scarce American
Portraits, Maps and Views

To be Sold in our Book Salesroom
Second Floor
Tuesday and Wednesday, December 15 and 16, 1891
Afternoon and Evening
Commencing at 2.30 P. M. and 8 P. M., each day

Catalogue compiled and Sale conducted by Stan. V. Henkels

Thos. Birch's Sons, Auctioneers
1110 Chestnut St., Phila.

Catalogue.

Washington Letters and other Papers.

1   Washington, **Gen'l Geo.** Autograph letter signed. Dated Mount Vernon, Sep. 20, 1785, addressed to Levi Hollingsworth, Esq., Philadelphia, with fine signature, on franked address. Folio, 2 pages.

"Sir:—

"Your letter of the 24th ult. did not get to my hands until the 17th inst., and then came by Post; for Mr. Jackson is an Inhabitant of Red Stone, 250 miles from me—I am obliged to him however for having taken notice of a wish of mine, which was accidentally expressed before him,—More so to you for having facilitated it,—and in a particular manner to Mr. Donaldson, for obligingly offering to carry it into effect.

"I have long been convinced, that the bed of the Potomac before my door, contains an inexhaustable fund of manure; and, if I could adopt an easy, simple, and expeditious method of raising, and taking it to the Land, that it may be converted to useful purposes—Mr. Donaldson's Hippopotamus, far exceeds any thing I had conceived with respect to the first; but wether the manner of its working will answer my purposes or not, is the question—By his using a horse, I fear it will not; as I shall have to go from one to eight hundred or 1000 yards from high water mark for the Mud, though I believe any quantity may be had at the lesser distance—The depth of water at the greater, will not exceed eight feet, and not much swell, unless the wind is turbulent. Under this information it would give me great satisfaction to have Mr. Donaldson's opinion of the utility of his Hippopotamus for my purposes; as mud, which is deep and soft, is to be raised at a distance from, and to be brought to the shore, when the tide is up, in vessel that draws but little water, and he would add to the favor (if the Machine is applicable to my wants) to inform me what kind of a Vessel is necessary for its operation—what would be the cost of this Vessel and of the Machine which is to be employed thereon—wether by a Model the whole could be constructed by good workmen here—or must be done under his own eye, and in that case, what would be the additional expense of bringing them from Philadelphia to this place?

"The kind offer of Mr. Donalson, for which I pray you to return him my sincere thanks, to furnish me with a model; or other information, and your obliging communication thereof, has drawn upon you both this trouble—instead therefor of making an apology for giving it, I will assure you both that I have a grateful sense of the kindness and am his &

"Yr Most Obed and
"Obliged Hble Serv't
"GEO WASHINGTON"

2 Washington, Gen'l Geo. Autograph Letter Signed. Dated Mount Vernon, Oct. 16, 1785. To Mr. A. Donaldson, Philadelphia, with fine signature on franked address. Folio.

"Sir :—

"Your letter of the first inst. did not reach my hands until last night, or I would have replied to it sooner.

"I am much obliged to you for the Model of your Hippopotamus, and the information which accompanied it,—I have a high expectation of its answering very valuable purposes, if the mud, in the beds of our Rivers, is of that fertilizing nature which the appearance indicate ; of which I mean to make a full experiment upon a small scale this fall, having the command of a flat bottom Boat, a scow, with which I can get out as much as will try the effect of different quantities upon small squares of exhausted Land, in all points similar—If the quantity of mud which shall be found necessary from this essay to dress land properly, when added to the expense of the Machine for raising it—bringing it to the Land,—cartage, &c &c does not come too high, I should certainly adopt the measure next year, and will then avail myself of the kind offer you have made me,—In the mean while, I pray you to accept my thanks for your politeness in this instance. I am Sir

"Yr Most Obed Hble Servt
"GEO WASHINGTON"

3 Washington. An Impression in Red Wax from the Seal of Gen'l Washington.

4 Washington. An Impression in Red Wax from the Watch Seal worn by Gen'l Washington.

Evacuation of New York.

5 Washington, Gen'l Geo. Letter signed, Head-Quarters, 10th June, 1783, to the Commissioners of Embarkation, in New York. Folio, 3 pages.

Relative to the Evacuation of New York. Extract—"That you would find embarrassments in the Execution of your Instructions, is no more than I expected—but to remove, is not so easy, as to forsee them—It is exceedingly difficult for me, not being a witness to the particular cases or acquainted with the circumstances which must fall under your view, in course of the Evacuation, to give you a precise definition or character of the Acts which you are to represent as infractions of the Treaty—nor can I undertake to give you an official construction of any particular expression, or Term, of the Treaty ; which must, in cases of ambiguity or different interpretation, be explained by the Sovereigns of the two Nations, or their Commissioners appointed for that purpose, as your Instructions from me, are given in consequence of the directions of Congress, and are grounded entirely on their Resolutions, which have been passed in compliance with Sir Guy Carleton's own application.—and for directing measures to be taken to obtain a DELIVERY of property in possession or under the Control of the British Troops, which latter case is not provided for by the articles of the Treaty,—I must be silent on the subject, leaving it to your own good Judgment and discretion, to execute your commission in the best manner you can, from a critical attention to the particular circumstances & acts which will fall under your knowledge, compared with the Terms of the Treaty, and the expressions of your instructions,—It however appears to me, that your reply to Mr. Elliot, was very pertinent and proper, for as the *power* is not in our Hands, it matters very little for us to devise modes, which we are not able to control, but which may be evaded by those who have the Execution, leaving to us the part only of remonstrating, without the means of prevention,—Indeed this observation may be said to apply to every Act to which your instructions will extend,—so that in fact I see little more that you will be able to do, than to be *witnesses* to the various Acts which will probably pass under your cognizance, in course of the Evacuation, wether they are the public acts of the Commander in Chief, or those of Individuals, and which, if you judge them to be infractions of either the Letter or the Spirit of the Treaty you are to represent to, and remonstrate against to Sir Guy Carleton, leaving it with him to give the redress, or involve such consequences as may be the result of the omission

"with great Regard & Esteem
"I am Gentlemen
"Your Most obedient and
"humble Servant
"GEO WASHINGTON"

6 Washington, Gen'l Geo. Autograph Receipt. Dated Mount Vernon, June 3, 1786. Small 4to.

Has signature in the body of the document. Also witnessed by Geo. A. Washington.

7 Washington, Gen'l Geo. Autograph Receipt. Dated Mount Vernon, Aug. 17, 1786. Small 4to.

Has signature in the body of the document.

8 Washington, Gen'l Geo. Autograph Receipt. Dated June 20, 1768. Small 4to.

Has signature in the body of the document.

9 Washington, Gen'l Geo. Autograph Statement of Cash to be received and paid by Col. F. Lewis. May, 1775. 4to, 2 pages.

Fine specimen of, and indexed in his handwriting on the back.

10 Washington, Gen'l Geo. Autograph Copy of a Patent granted to Jno. Ball for 300 acres of land on Doeg's Run, 8th March, 1799. Folio.

Fine specimen of Washington's handwriting.

11 Washington, Gen'l Geo. Autograph Postscript of Five Lines, to a letter written by Sam'l Irwin to Col. Jno. Augustine Washington. Dated Washington County, Penna., Sept. 6, 1782. 4to.

12 Washington, Col. Geo. Autograph Letter to by Robert Adams. No place. No date. 4to.

Indexed on the back in Washington's handwriting.

13 Washington, Gen'l Geo. Autograph Letter to, by Edmund Randolph. Marked private. No place. No date. 4to.

14 Washington, Gen'l Geo. Autograph Letter to, by Geo. W. Fairfax. Dated Yorktown, Aug. 5, 1773. 4to, 3 pages.
Indexed on the back in Washington's handwriting.

15 Washington, Gen'l Geo. Autograph Letter to, by James Maury. Dated Liverpool, Dec. 26, 1795. 4to, 3 pages.
Indexed on the back in Washington's handwriting.

16 Washington ——. The Estate of General Washington, deceased, in account with Clement Biddle. Dated Philadelphia, Sept. 24, 1801, and signed by Clement Biddle. Also autograph letter signed from Col. Clement Biddle, in reference to the above; to which is added a receipt in full for the amount of his claim against Gen'l Washington's Estate. Dated Philadelphia, Oct. 17, 1801. 4to, 2 pieces.

17 Washington Estate. Deed of Sale from Matthew Thompson to Charles Rose for land in Stafford County, Virginia. Dated March 14, 1688. 4to.

18 Washington Estate. Lease from Hon. Geo. W. Fairfax to Peter Dillon for a tract of land called "Shannandale" in Berkeley County, Va. Dated March 20, 1786. 4to.

19 Washington Estate. Lease from Wm. Spencer to John Manly for 100 acres of land in Prince William County, Va. Dated Oct. 23, 1738. 4to.

20 Washington Estate. Lease and Release from George Harrison to John Manly for land in Fairfax County, Va. Dated May 15, 1744. 4to. 2 pieces.

21 Washington Estate. Lease and Release from Thos. Marshall to John Manly for land in Prince George County, Maryland. Dated May 10, 1744. 4to. 2 pieces.

22 **Washington Estate.** Lease and Release from John Manly and wife to Dan'l French for land in Fairfax County, Va. Dated Aug. 30, 1746. 4to. 2 pieces.

Each indexed on the back in the handwriting of Gen'l Washington.

23 **Washington Estate.** Lease and Release from John Posey and wife to Dan'l French for land in Fairfax County, Va. Dated June 16, 1760. Folio. 2 pieces.

Each indexed on the back in the handwriting of Gen'l Washington.

24 **Washington Estate.** Lease and Release from George Harrison and wife to Lawrence Washington for land in Prince William County, Va. Dated Nov. 20, 1739. 4to. 2 pieces.

25 **Custis, Nelly.** Adopted Daughter of Gen'l Washington. Autograph letters signed to Mrs. Wolcott. Dated Mount Vernon, March 19, 1797. 4to. 2 pages.

The letter was written immediately upon her arrival at Mount Vernon from Philadelphia at the expiration of Gen'l Washington's second term as President. We quote a few paragraphs: "Grandmamma informs me that you wished me to write & inform you how we are after our Journey, I have therefore taken pen in hand to do so & also to thank you for the kind interest you have ever taken in our welfare. We arrived here on Wednesday, without any accident, after a tedious and fatiguing journey of seven days, The roads were better than we expected to find them, although in some parts were bad. * * * * * * * Grandpapa is very well & much pleased with being once more *Farmer Washington*. I am perfectly well and happy in returning to this place & to my Dear relations, although I shall always remember with affection & regret those Friends left in Philadelphia."

Written on Gen'l Washington's water marked paper.

26 **Washington Estate.** Plan of a Plot of Land on Dogue Run. 4to.

27 **Hand, Gen'l Edward.** Autograph Letters signed to Col. David Humphreys, Aid to Gen'l Washington. (So addressed.) Dated New Windsor, Oct. 16, 1783. 8vo. 2 pages.

Complaining of the injustice done him in not settling his account and praying that he may not again fall in the hands of sharpers. He further says: "Present my and Mrs. Hand's most respectful compliments to Gen'l Washington and the Gentlemen of the Family."

Returns from The American Revolutionary Army, during the early stages of the War.

At Pluckemin and New Milford.

28   A Collection of papers consisting of Returns and Invoices of Military Stores, Pay Rolls, Receipts for Money and Ammunition, etc., for the Revolutionary Army whilst stationed at Pluckemin and New Milford, 1778–1779. All signed by the persons in authority at the time. 46 pieces.

At Fort Schuyler.

29   Returns of Ammunition and Artillery Stores in the Magazine at Fort Schuyler, for June 1 and July 1, 1777, and January 20, and March 1, 1778. Three signed by Capt. Jos. Savage, and one by Lieut. Isaiah Thompson. Oblong, 4to. 4 pieces.

At Bennington.

30   Receipt for Ordnance stores. Bennington, 29th October, 1777. Signed by Jos. Fay. 4to.

At White Plains.

31   Return of Military Stores under the care of Samuel French, Esq., Commissary, White Plains, August 1, 1778. Signed by Rich'd Frothingham, D. C. M. S. Oblong, 4to, and Invoice of Military Stores, by Jos. Watkin, C. O. and M. Stores to camp at White Plains. Lebanon, Aug. 27, 1778. Signed by Jos. Watkin. Folio, 3 pages. 2 pieces.

At Stillwater.

32   Returns of Ammunition and Ordnance at Camp Stillwater. Dated Sep. 22, 23, 26 and 29th, and Oct. 8, 1777. Signed by Lieut. Wm. Price, Lieut. Jos. Perry, Lieut. Thos. Vose, Benj. Egbert, Capt. Stephen Buckland, Capt. Jas. Furneval and Benj. Bartlett. 4to and oblong 4to. 8 pieces.

At Danbury.

33   Return of Ordnance Stores remaining on hand at Danbury, Dec. 8, 1778. Signed by Andrew Comstock in behalf of Lambert Lockwood, Commander of Military and Ordnance Stores, and various Receipts for Moneys to Sam'l Hodgdon, signed by the various Commanders of Military Stores at that Point. Dated, Danbury, Nov. 17 and 29, Dec. 4th, 9th, 10th, 11th, 18th and 23d, 1778. 11 pieces.

At Fishkill.

34   Returns of Ordnance and Stores at Fishkill, and on Board of Magazine Sloop at Fishkill Landing, 1778-1779. Signed by Jasp. Maud Gedley, Geo. Marvin, John Ruddock and other Conductors of Military Stores. 4to and folio. 7 pieces.

At Stony Point.

35   Return of Ordnance taken at Stony Point, July 16, 1779, and Return of the Ammunition remaining at Stony Point July 17, 1779. Signed by Wm. Pennington, C. M. S. 4to and folio. 2 pieces.

36   Remains of Ordnance and Stores on Stony Point, June 1770. Including that Received from his Majesty's ship Renown. 7 pages, folio.

   A British Invoice of Stores captured at that place.

At Boston.

37   Receipt from Payne Downs to Sam'l Hodgdon, for Pay and Subsistance for Dec., Jan. and Feb'y, 1779. Invoice of Six Barrels of Flour sent to Boston, etc. 4 pieces.

At Fredericksburgh.

38 Return of the Ordnance and Military Stores at Camp Fredericksburgh. Oct. 9 and Nov. 9, 1778. Signed by J. Giles, C. M. S. Oblong 4to, 2 pieces.

At Farmington, Connecticut.

39 Return of Ordnance and Ordnance Stores at Farmington, in the State of Connecticut. Jan. 20, Feb. 13, Feb. 15, March 18, April 2 and April 27, 1778. Signed by Benj. Bartlett, C. O. and M. S. Folio, 7 pieces.

At the Highlands.

40 Return of Artillery and Stores in Camp at the Pass in the Highlands. June 6, 1778. Signed by Andrew Moodie, Captain of Artillery. 4to.

At Lebanon.

41 Lebanon, June 30, 1779. Invoice of Musket Cartridges sent to Major Sam'l Hodgdon, C. M. Stores at New Windsor, on the Hudson River, by George Ingles, C. M. Stores at Lebanon, in the care of Wm. Cook, C. M. Stores. Signed by Wm. Cook. 2 pages.

At Peekskill.

42 Return of Ordnance Stores at Peekskill. June 26 and Sept. 2, 1778. Signed by Thos. Gray, C. M. S. Oblong and small 4to, 3 pieces.

At Ticonderoga.

43 Return of Stores sent to Ticonderoga. Signed by Nath'l Barber, Jr., D. C. M. S., at Boston, Feb. 19, 1777. 3 pages, folio.
    Stained and worn.

Col. Stevens' Corps of Artillery.

44 Park, White Plains, July 20, 1778. A return of all ammunition wagons, baggage wagons and pieces of ordnance and tumble carts belonging to Col. (Ebenezer)

Stevens' Corps of Artillery, now present in the Park, and a return of the ammunition and implements of war in Capt. Wm. Johnston's detachment in Major Ebenezer Steven's Corps of Artillery . . . . . . Camp Stillwater, Sept. 22, 1777. Signed by Capt. Wm. Johnston. 4to, 2 pieces.

45   Letter signed by (Col.) Ebenezer Stevens. Dated Camp, Sept. 26, 1777. Folio.

An interesting letter in relation to making returns of the ordnance and stores at Ticonderoga, for Gen'ls Gates and Knox and Congress, and giving the general instructions for collecting all the paper of old books and accounts of merchants, lead, and other articles that may be necessary to keep the laboratory going for the manufacture of cartridges.

46   Invoice of Ammunition and Implements for Two brass 12 pdrs. to join the Park at Chester, west side of North River. June 22, 1779. Signed by J. Hubbell.

47   Autograph Receipt. Signed by Sam'l Hodgdon, C. of O. S., for his and Lieut. Ingersol's expenses to Boston, as per order of Major Gen'l Schuyler to forward on Cannon and Stores, together with the Memorandum book of the Expenses of the Trip, in the handwriting of Sam'l Hodgdon. 2 pieces.

At Albany.

48   Return of Ammunition and Artillery Stores in store in Albany this 1st April, 1777. Signed by P. V. Rensalaer, Keeper of Stores. Invoice of Ordnance Stores sent to Albany to Philip Van Rancilier, Commissary of Military Stores, by order of Maj. Gen. Gates, Aug. 27, 1777. Signed at Springfield by Col. Ezek. Cheever. Copy of the Return of Ordnance Stores sent Albany since 10th July, 1777. Signed at Springfield Aug 24, 1777, by Col. Ezek. Cheever, and six Receipts for Ammunition, Money, etc. Signed by Lieut. Col. John Popkin, of the Park Artillery, Sam'l Hodgdon, D. C. of O. S., Enos Hitchcock, and others. Folio and small 4to. 9 pieces.

49   Invoice of Cannon Powder sent to Headquarters, Sep. 8th, 1779, under the care of Mr. Schutz, C. M. S., by order of James Pearson, C. M. S., in Philadelphia. Signed at Washingtonsburgh by Wm. Schutz. Folio.

50 Invoice of Sundry Military Stores received from Philadelphia July 6, 1779, under the charge of Mr. Wm. Schutz, C. M. S. Signed by Samuel Hodgdon. 4to.

51 Return of Arms, Accoutrements, etc., Wanting in the 2d Penna. Brigade, commanded by Thos. Craig, Esq., Colonel, July 11, 1779. Signed by Col. T. Craig. A Return of Ammunition and Implements belonging to a Six Pounder that Capt. Sargent is supplied with, Aug. 1778. Signed by Lieut. James Hall. Encouragement for Blacksmiths to serve in the Corps of Artillery under Major Ebenezer Stevens. Signed by Major Ebenezer Stevens, Thos. Patten and Boylston Patten, etc. Folio and 4to. 5 pieces.

52 Pay Abstract for the Armors that are with the Military Stores of the United States for December, 1778, together with their receipts for their month's pay, to Sam'l Hodgdon, G. M. S. Invoice of Sundry Articles on board the Schooner "Sally," Captain Langdons. Return of Ordnance Stores in the upper Laboratory on Mount Independence, April 17, 1777. Invoice of Military Stores Remaining on hand from Gen. Lee's Division, Aug. 20, 1778, and other papers of the same character. Folio and 4to. 20 pieces.

53 Interesting Letters Written by Eminent Characters connected with the Government during the American Revolution, written from 1776 to 1785, as also a letter from Matthew Elliot, dated Pittsburgh, September 15, 1774, noticing Lord Dunmore's expedition against the Shawnese Indians; in all, 9 pieces. 4to and folio.

54 Heron, Capt. Jas., Prisoner in the Hands of the British. Two autograph letters, signed. Dated New Utrecht, Long Island, Jan'y 30 and March 29, 1778. Folio. 2 pieces.

    Complaining of his not having friends to intercede for his exchange, and the rascally treatment received at the hands of the British Commissary of Prisoners.

55 Manuscript Copy of an Ordinance for Regulating the Treasury and adjusting the Public Accounts. By the United States in Congress assembled, Sept. 11, 1781. Signed by Geo. Bond, Depy. Sec. Folio. 2 pages.

56 Manuscript Resolves of the Board of Treasury respecting a dispute between Gen. Gates and the Commissioners of Accounts in the Northern Department. Dated Treasury Office, Phila., Aug. 27, 1777. Signed by Wm. Govett, also Remarks on some of the Warrants Drawn by Gen. Gates, through which the dispute arose. Folio, 2 pieces.

57 Manuscript Resolutions of Congress. Authorizing the Payment of the allowance due various Deputy Commissary Generals, as well as Elias Boudenot, as well as the commissions for settling the accounts of the Army in the Northern Department. Dated Phila., March 15, 1777 and May 9, 1777. Signed by Wm. Houston, Dep. Sec. Folio, 3 pages.

58 Col. John Cadwalader's Regiment, Third Battalion of Philadelphia Associates, July 11 to July 18, 1776, at Camp Trenton, N. J. Return of Arms, Ammunition, Accoutrements, Provisions, Men, etc. Signed by Lieut. Alex. Fullerton, Capt. Ferguson McElwaine, Lieut. Hugh Lennox, Capt. Jos. Falconer, Capt. Geo. Henry and Lieut. Alex. Nesbitt. 4to, 8 pieces.

59 Capt. Sharp Delany's Company, Third Batalion of Philadelphia Associates, July 14 to 17, 1776, at Camp Trenton, N. J. Returns of Provisions, Orders for Rations and Sundries Needed. Signed by Lieut. Wm. Turnbull. Small 4to, 5 pieces.

60 Returns of the Various Companys in the Third Batalion of Philadelphia Associates, as also memorandums of Sundries Needed, at Camp Trenton, N. J., July 12 to 19, 1776, Commanded by Capt. Henry, Capt. Semple, Capt. Jos. Falconer, Capt. Francis Gurney, Capt. Elias Boys, and Capt. Thos. Fitzsimmons. 26 pieces.

Revolutionary Army Receipt Book.

61 Receipt Book of the Quarter-Master of the Third Battalion of Philadelphia Militia, July 17, 1776, containing Receipts for Military Supplies, signed by Col. John Cadwalader, Capt. Francis Gurney, Capt. Sharp Delany, Capt. Jos. Falconer, Capt. Wm. Semple, Capt. Ferguson McElwaine, Capt. Elias Boys and Ensign Gavin Hamilton. 4to.

Revolutionary Manuscript Documents.

62 Gen'l Schuyler's Account Current of Specie Recieved and Disbursed on Account of the United States. Dated Feb. 23, 1777, a true contemporary copy in the Handwriting of one of the Auditors of the Treasury. 4 pages folio.

63 List of the Debts and Credits of the Undermentioned Men of His Majesty's 20th Regiment of Foot. Draughted into the 55th Regiment at New York, the 24th Aug., 1778. Charlottesville, Virginia, 20th May, 1779. Signed, W. R. Gilbert, P. M., 20th. A true contemporary copy "*from the original which was intercepted by and is now in the hands of Col. Bland, at Charlottesville.*" Folio.

64 List of Accounts taken from the Commissioners' Books at Albany, April 15, 1777. A True Transcript made by one of the Auditors of the Treasury, wherein Gen'l Benedict Arnold is charged with $16,988.02. Gen'l Rich. Montgomery with $42,507.02. Col. Anthony Wayne with $9,000, etc. 3 pages folio.

<small>The paper upon which this account is written, is a rarity in itself, as it bears the water mark of the Independence Bell, and name of one the earliest American manufacturers.</small>

65 Journal and Ledger of Jonathan Trumbull, D. P. M. General's account to the settlement made the 28th January, 1777. (This includes the accounts at Albany from Dec. 2, 1776, to Jan. 20, 1777.) A true transcript in the handwriting of one of the Auditors of the Treasury. 19 pages, folio.

66 An Account of Moneys Advanced by Jonathan Trumbull, Jr., Esq., Paymaster-General in the Northern Department for Recruiting Service. A true contemporary copy in the handwriting of one of the Auditors of the Treasury from the original in the Auditor's Office, Albany, 12th May, 1777. 3 pages, folio.

67 Account of Pay Due to Capt. Michael Schmyser's Company (of the Flying Camp) of Col. Swoop's Battalion during the time they were Prisoners; also the sums stopped from them for Capt. Schmyser and the cash actually paid them by the Commissioners, together with Capt. Michael Schmyser's Receipt for the same. Dated at Yorktown, June 25, 1778. 3 pages, folio.

68 A Contemporary Copy of the Speech made and delivered in writing by Mr. St. Clair, Prothonitor or Clerk of the Court of Westmoreland County, in the Province of Pennsylvania, and his associates, the Justices of the said County, to the Militia of the Colony of Virginia assembled at Fort Pitt by order of his Excellency, the Earl of Dunmore, Governor of the said Colony, on Tuesday, Jan'y 25, 1774, with remarks on the same. 7 pages, folio.

Interesting document relating to the early history of Pittsburgh.

69 Account of Moneys Loaned in the Different States from the opening of the Loan Offices to the 1st March, 1778, and bearing interest in Bills of Exchange on France, with the amount of one year's interest on the sum loaned in each respective State, in the handwriting of one of the Auditors of the Treasury. Folio.

70 Estimate of Moneys Loaned to the United States at certain periods and reduced to specie value by the Table of Depreciation. Dated at the Auditor General's Office, February 16, 1781. Folio.

71 The Estate of the late Major-Gen'l Montgomery in account with the United States, July 29 to Dec. 23, 1775. Dated Albany, March 26, 1777. A true transcript by one of the Auditors of the Treasury. Folio.

72 Return of Provisions at Sundry Posts in the Northern Department *vs.* Ticonderoga, Bennington, Skeensborough, Fort Ann, Fort George, Albany, German Flats, and Johnstown. Dated Albany, 13th March, 1777, and signed by Elisha Avery, D. C. Gen'l. Folio.

73 Surrender of Burgoyne. Instruction from the Board of Treasury to the Commissioner for settling the accounts of the Convention Troops. Signed by Robt. Troup, Sec'y. Dated Philadelphia, June 23, 1779. Copy of a report to the Board of Treasury respecting Gen'l Phillips and the Convention Troops. Dated Aug. 30, 1779, in the handwriting of the Commissioner. Folio, 2 pieces.

74 Surrender of Burgoyne. A Contemporary Copy of the Articles of Convention between Lieut.-Gen'l Burgoyne and Major-Gen'l Gates, dated Camp at Saratoga, Oct. 16, 1777. Folio, 3 pages, and a List of the British Troops of the Convention of Saratoga, Oct. 1, 1778. Signed by Thos. Bibby, D. A. Gen'l. 4to, 2 pieces.

75 Lord Howe's Germantown Proclamation. A Contemporary Copy of the Proclamation by his Excellency, Sir Wm. Howe, at Germantown, Sept. 28, 1777, granting protection to all who shall return and remain peaceably at their usual place of abode. Folio.

76 Sir Guy Carleton's Proclamation at Detroit, June 24, 1777. A Contemporary Copy of a Proclamation found with the bodies of three soldiers killed by the Wyandot Indians at the Kettaning, Aug. 1777. Folio.

77 A Collection of Revolutionary Documents. Contemporary Copies of Letters and Documents, Government Accounts, etc., issued by and to one of Commissioners for adjusting the accounts with the Treasury during the Revolution. 35 pieces.

78 **Letters Written by Jno. Carter, Assistant Commissioner** for settling the accounts with the Army in the Northern Department. Dated Albany, April 8, 1777, June 25, 1777, July 3, 1777, Aug. 7, 1777, and Aug. 10, 1777, and White Plains, Sept. 9, 1778. 6 pieces, folio.

Containing interesting news relative to the evacuation of Fort Ticonderoga and Mount Independence, and to the movements of the army under St. Clair, Schuyler and British forces under Burgoyne.

79 **Early Pittsburgh Document. The Original Manuscript Memorial** to Congress and to the President of the State, of certain persons requesting the removal of Col. Brodhead, to wit.:

"Pittsburgh 9th May 1781.

"Sir

Our remote situation here subjects us to many heavy Greivances, as well as Inconveniences, we have bore up under them with Fortitude, Patience & Perseverance, till we find ourselves in a Manner crushed into Complaint, We find ourselves at last compelled with our Fellow Citizens in this Town, and County of Westmoreland, to Remonstrate to Congress, and the President and Council of the State, for the removal of Colonel Brodhead from his Command, our happiness, and the Tranquility of this Country, depends on the success of our Remonstrance, We know your disposition to oblige, as well as your feelings for those in our Situation; Insulted and Injured by those whose duty it is to afford us protection, and we therefore hope you will so far oblige us on this occasion, as to wait on the President of Congress, as also the Pre'dt of the State, and present to them, the respective Packets which accompanies this Letter, which will be returned a very singular favor, and much oblige, Sir.

Your Most Obd't Humble Serv'ts

JOHN ORMSBY, DEVEREUX SMITH A. FOWLER,
              JOHN IRWIN   EDW'D WARD,
              THOS SMALLMAN   ROBT CAMPBELL."

Folio, 2 pages.

80 **Muhlenberg, Gen'l Peter. Autograph Letter, Signed,** to Brig. Gen'l Knox. Dated May 21, 1779. 4to, 2 pages.

EXTRACT.—"I have sent my Sword to Philadelphia to have it repaired, but it has been shuffled about so long, that I have lost it, and am now without one altogether, I understand Gen'l Knox has some for the Artillery officers & tho I cannot in the strict sense of the word, be comprehended in that number yet I wish in the present case to be included in the return, if it can be done with propriety. If I cannot obtain one, on any other terms. I will promise to return it, as soon as I can get another."

81 **Knox, Gen'l Henry. An Estimate of Stores wanting** for the present Campaign, 1779. Signed by Gen'l Henry Knox and Sam'l Hodgdon. 4to, 2 pages.

82 **Hodgdon, Sam'l. Original Draft of a Letter, signed** to Maj. Gen'l Heath. Dated Sept. 1, 1777. 4to, 2 pages.

EXTRACT.—"It is with pleasure I can inform your honor that Col. Morgan has arrived and joined our camp with several hundred Riflemen. The Militia daily coming, and a prospect of advancing animates the whole, I have taken the liberty to inclose your honor a Return of Stores taken from the Enemy at Fort Schuyler."

83 Wilkinson, Gen'l Jas. A Return of Drums and Fifes Wanting for the Corps of Artillery under the command of Maj. Ebenezer Stevens, Van Schaick's Island, Aug. 29, 1777. Signed by Stephen Buckland, Capt. Artillery, together with an autograph order signed by J. Wilkinson, D. A. Gen'l, for the above fifes and drums. Small 4to.

84 Physick, Edmund. Receipt signed. Dated Philad., March 4, 1775. Small 4to.

Military Stores sent to the Army under Washington.

85 Invoice of Ammunition and Military Stores sent by Col. Benj. Flower, Com. Gen. Milt. Stores, to Sam'l Hodgdon, Esq., Field Com'y Milt'y Stores with the Main Army under the command of his Excellency, Gen'l Washington, June 21, 1779, signed by Wm. Schutz, Conductor of Military Stores. Folio, 2 pages.

86 Invoice of Iron Ball, 18-pounders sent by Col. Benjamin Flower, Com'y Gen'l Mil'y Stores, July 7, 1779, to Sam'l Hodgdon, Esq., Field Com'y Mil'y Stores at the park of Artillery with the Main Army under the command of his Excellency, Gen'l Washington. Signed by Jno. Jlan, Military Conductor. Folio.

87 Invoice of Empty 8-inch Shells and Empty 5½-inch shells sent by Col. Benj. Flower, Com'y Gen'l Milit'y Stores, July 13, 1779, to Sam'l Hodgdon, Esq., Field Com'y Milit'y Stores with the Main Army under the command of his Excellency, Gen'l Washington. Signed by Henry Dechert, Wagon Master.

88 Invoice of Cannon and Carriages, etc., sent by Col. Benj. Flower, Com'y Gen'l Mil'y Stores, to Samuel Hodgdon, Esq., Field Com'y Mil'y Stores, with the Main Army under the command of his Excellency, Gen'l Washington. Signed by J. Pearson, Com'y Mil'y Stores. Folio.

89 Invoice of Military Stores sent by Col. Benj. Flower, Com'y Gen'l Mil'y Stores, to Sam'l Hodgdon, Esq., Field Com'y Mil'y Stores with the main army under the command of his Excellency, General Washington, Sept. 11, 1779. Signed J. Pearson, Com'y Mil'y Stores, and Jas. Lucas, Wagon Master. Folio.

90 Invoice of Iron Cannon, 12-pounders, sent by Col. Benj. Flower, Commissary General Military Stores, to Sam'l Hodgdon, Esq., Field Com. Mil'y Stores with the main army under the command of his Excellency, Gen'l Washington, Sept. 13, 1779. Signed by J. Pearson, Com. Mil'y Stores, and Henry Baker, Conductor of Military Stores. Folio.

91 Invoice of Powder and Musket Cartridges sent by Col. Benj. Flower, Com'y Gen'l Mil'y Stores, to Sam'l Hodgdon, Esq., Field Com'y Mil'y Stores with the main army under the command of his Excellency Gen'l Washington, Aug. 19, 1779. Signed by Henry Seleir, Wagon Master. Folio.

92 Invoice of Cannon Ball, 18-pounders, sent by Col. Benj. Flower, Com'y Gen'l Mil'y Stores, to Sam'l Hodgdon, Esq., Field Com'y Mil'y Stores with the main army under command of his Excellency, Gen'l Washington, Sept. 24, 1779. Signed by Dan'l Hamil, Wagon Master. Folio.

93 Washington. Bookplate of Judge Bushrod Washington. Original impression. Small 4to.

94 Clay Henry. Autograph Letter Signed Washington, 1st April, 1825, to Judge Bushrod Washington. 8vo.

Extract. "Allow me to present to you Mr. Jouett a native of K. artist who is charged by the legislature of that state to take the portrait of La Fayette. He wishes to associate with the principal figure some scenes drawn from Mount Vernon. I pray you to allow him the privilege of taking them, and to receive him, as he is, a gentleman of honor and high respectability."

95 Hamilton, Alex. Autograph Letter Signed, to Sharp Delany, Treasury Department, July 31, 1790; together with Signature on Franked address. 4to, 2 pages.

96 Colonial Paper Money. 1 Four-shilling Piece, dated Jan. 1, 1776, printed by Jas. Adams, 1776. 1 Five-shilling Piece, dated Jan. 1, 1776, printed by Jas. Adams, 1776. 1 Six-shilling Piece, dated Jan. 1, 1776.

printed by Jas. Adams, 1776. 1 Ten-shilling Piece, dated Jan. 1, 1776, printed by Jas. Adams, 1776. 1 Ten shilling Piece, dated June 18, 1764, printed by B. Franklin and D. Hall, 1764. 1 Thirty-shilling Piece, dated April 25, 1776, printed by Hall and Sellers, 1776, 1 Twenty-shilling Piece, dated Oct. 1, 1773, printed by Hall and Sellers; and 1 Twenty-shilling Piece dated Jan. 18, 1764, printed by B. Franklin and D. Hall, 1764, together with an impression of one of the First United States Revenue Stamps (50c.) on a promissory note dated Jan. 26, 1814, together. 10 pieces.

In good clean condition.

Important Revolutionary Correspondence.

97 **Wells, John.** The Revolutionary Correspondence of, as Commissioner for settling the accounts with the Army of the Northern Department, narrating the cabal against General Washington, displaying the selfishness and arrogance of Generals Gates and Arnold, as coming under his personal observation, Describing the Various Victories and Defeats of the Army in New York and Vermont, including the Evacuation of Fort Ticonderoga and Fort Ann, Battle of Bennington, The Surrender of Burgoyne, The Massacre of Scholarie, and Cherry Valley, etc. The correspondence is dated at Albany and takes in the Period between May 12th, 1777, and March 7, 1779, in all 35 letters, forming the most interesting collection that has come under our observation for many years. The letters are mostly addressed to Jas. Milligan, Commissioner for Accounts, at Philadelphia.

1st.—Dated Albany, May 12, 1777. A Personal Letter asking for information of his late friend, Mr. A. Bonfield.

2d.—Dated Great Banington, May 28, 1777: "Mr. Dean, the Interpreter is come down and has been with him the Sachems and Chief Warriors of the 6 Nations, amongst which are some Indians from Canada. They were on the Road before Major Vernimet & his party got up to Fort Schuyler, so, that scheme has not taken place," * * * "I find we must be very circumspect in all we advance, for a day or two before I left Albany going to Gen. Gates on business, found them at Table after dinner with comp'y, he began by extolling us in the highest manner for our Vigilance, care,

Integrity & the like, saying we were right to represent his having exceeded the Salary allowed by Congress to his Secretary, as when we made it, we could not know, that he was authorized to do it, & he was glad to find we made no distinction, but then ag'n we had represented that he had paid acco'ts by his Warrant on the paymaster, which acco'ts had been examined by Committees of Officers appointed by him, & which officers were interested in said acco'ts. Therefore as Gen Wayne, & Sinclair were the persons generally appointed by him, it was their affair, and when Gen. Sinclair arrives he should acquaint him with the letter he had received from Mr. Hillegas on that subject & if he thought proper to Crop our Ears, he might. I cannot say but the expression struck me coming from a Commander in Chief, & spit sticks in my stomach, a very poetic expression before strangers, or even his own family, on a subject matter of public business." 2 pages, folio.

3d.—Dated Albany, June 9, 1777, on Public affairs: "Cannot understand upon what plan Congress has promised the Canadian Volunteers, who have remained the whole time at Phila & about and done no service 103 Dollars each without Discrimination, * * * for while they get money for nothing it cannot be expected they will do any Duty." 1 page folio.

4th.—Dated Albany, June 27, 1777. "Those Canadians who were sent to Canada are returned * * * They inform us Burgoyne arrived at Quebec the 10th May without any Troops * * * we have heard of the retreat to Brunswick & as it is said, of that place being evacuated & in our possession." 1 page folio.

5th.—Dated Albany, July 5th, 1777. "We have been set in motion here by the Enemies arrival at Crown Point, & sending a strong party up Otter Creek & another round to cut off the Communication, we have heard various reports of attacks & repulses. They have however cut off the communication to Ty, by way of Lake Geo; as they are at the Landing, we had time to get back to Fort Geo; all the Prov's that was not over the carrying place & to Burn the Block House & Saw Mills before they got possession of Mount Hope. Gen'l Sinclair with his Troops are in high spirits by an Express arrived this morning, and the Militia are marching up. There is a report that the Enemy attacked the Lines on Thursday & were beat off. * * * * * The Free Masons had a Dinner at Dennistons late Vernons, he charged 12/ a head eating and 16/ a bottle wine, what will be the end of these things. Hewetson a half-pay officer was yesterday Executed at 12 O'clock, agreeable to the sentence of a Gen'l Court Martial of the Militia, contrary to the opinion of the Tories." 1 page, folio.

6th.—Dated Albany, July 10th, 1777. "Your two favours of the 23d ulto, came to hand the 7th Curr't the day we got a report of the loss of Ticonderoga and Mount Independence, without a single circumstance of consequence not easily credited, but at night Col Hay, D. Q. M. Gen'l. who was the last off the Ground & had left Fort Ann that morning arrived, by him we got an Acco't that the Evacuation of those posts was made the most sudden, and with the greatest precipitation and confusion, after a Counsel of War of the Gen'l Officers, to the great regret of the Army who were in high Spirits, & enraged at leaving every thing behind them. Gen'l St Clair retreated with the Main Body of the Garrison by the way of Castle Town & as yet has not been heard of this way; * * * * * * As Winslow has left the pay office & the Artillery, Pierce got up just in time to secure the Military Chest & public papers which Winslow had caused to be put into one of the Battoes, as for giving you any Distinct particulars it is impossible, every one it Thunder Struck, we have lost all our Cannon, Ammunition, Stores, Prov's. Medicines & baggage Tents, Boats and Vessels. * * * * If Gen'l Schuyler can but collect a respectable Army of Continental Troops & Militia at Fort Edward this County may be Saved, otherwise nothing can prevent their forming a junction if Gen'l Howe comes up. * * * * * Oh for some Virginia Rifle Men. Col Morgans Reg't would be of great use this way." 3 pages, folio.

7th.—Dated Albany, July 19, 1777. "Gen'l Schuyler with some Continentals & all the Militia are at Fort Edward putting a stop to the Progress of Burgoyne & I hope when we get up the re-inforcement now on the March, we shall be able to make head against them at any rate, The loss of the Stores, Money & Public Acco'ts will be terrible relative to our Departments." 1 page, folio.

8th.—Dated Albany, July 21, 1777. Giving another long and detailed account of the evacuation of Ticonderoga and Mount Independence, correcting some errors in the letter of July 10th, and narrating the shameful behavior of Major Nicholson, also mentioning the arrival of Gen'l Arnold. 3 pages, 4to.

9th.—Dated Albany, Aug. 4, 1777. "Our Army is at Still-water having left Saratoga and Burgoyne has issued another thundering Proclamation." 1 page, 4to.

10th.—Dated Albany, Aug. 4, 1777, complaining of not being properly supported by Congress, as also regretting that certain letters of his had been published. 1 page, 4to.

11th.—Dated Albany, Aug. 8, 1777. A long and interesting letter relating the shameful treatment he received at the hands of Gen'l Gates, and complaining of the manner in which he has been slandered for strictly performing his duty. 3 pages, folio.

12th.—Dated Albany, Aug. 14, 1777. "I dare say I need not urge you to push the absolute necessity of our being allowed Rations, in fact we have as much right to them as others in the public service, & when the Commiss' for the Middle Department joined Genl Washington, altho they did no business, on acco't of the confused State of affairs the Genl ordered the Commissary Genl to supply them with what Prov's &c they were in want of. * * * * Genl Arnold is now in town going to the Westward & Phil Ransalaer this moment tells me our Northern Army is moving down to half Moon." 1 page, folio.

13th.—Dated Albany, Aug. 19, 1777. Speaking of an interview that he and Mr. Carter had with Gen'l Gates relative to his charge against them of representing falsehoods to the Treasury, and containing interesting news of which we quote from his own writing: " Genl Gates arrived with re-inforcements of the 2 Reg'ts Livingston's & Courtland's, with the Militia of this State, I hope will make us look back again, Yesterday we had an acco't of a Battle on the Grants, that we had taken near 500 Pris'rs & 4 Brass field pieces, which is confirmed this Morning, on the 16th Genl Stark with a Body of about 2000 Men mostly Militia fell in with a body of the Enemy of about 1500 who came with the design to possess themselves of Bennington, he attacked them in their Entrenchments & beat them out of one after the other & totally defeated them, they had 4 Brass field pieces which fell into our hands, with a Great deal of Baggage, 1 Lieut Col, 1 Major, 5 Capts, 12 Lieuts. 4 Ensigns, 2 Cornets, 1 Judge Adv, 2 Canadian Officers, 3 Surgeons, 37 British Soldiers, 398 Hessians, 38 Canadians, 151 Tories, so wounded taken Prisoners & about 200 dead on the field, we had 30 killed and about 50 wounded, Genl Lincoln joined our people after the action with a reinforcement, This acco't is by a letter from Genl Lincoln, the prisoners are sent to Massachusetts State, This is an Event happy & important, executed with great Spirit & Bravery & with a very inconsiderable loss on our side, we daily expect something decisive from the westward, if the enemy have but Courage to stand their ground, on our peoples approach, I blush to mention our Grand Army, until they turn their faces to the Enemy. * * * * You have doubtless seen Col Wilkinson's Letter to the Printer on the Boston paper 11th Aug. it is the copy of himself and explains in some measure what I wanted to say in one of my letters to to you, on people of his Stamp, I think it can do him no honour or Service, inter nos." 2 pages, 4to.

14th.—Dated Albany, Sept. 6, 1777. On business affairs. 1 page, folio.

15th.—Dated Albany, Sept. 9, 1777. "I have no reason to Contradict the news to the Westward as wrote you, except perhaps that Sir John Johnson is reported not killed, as imagined, but as to the Indians, they have lost most of their Chief Warriours, & as I was fearfull, Genl St Leidger Decamped on the approach of Genl Arnold with a reinforcement to the Garrison of Fort Schuyler (Stanwix) the Enemy cannonaded & threw shells into the fort with great fury, from 11 to three in the afternoon, during which time they were retreating, on ceasing their fire, they drew off their Artillery unperceived by the Garrison who had no information, either of Genl Arnolds approach or their retreat, until a Deserter came in, which they suspected but two more coming in with an Indian called Hanniost Schuyler, who had been made prisoner with Walter Butler as a Spy & had been set at Liberty by Genl Arnold on a promise he would get into the Fort & also on his way acquaint the Enemy that a reinforcement of 3000 men was at hand, which he says he did, & which determined them to retreat. The matter being confirmed without a doubt, Col Gansevoort sent out a party of 70 men in pursuit of them, who came up with the Artillery Men just as they had got the 4 Royals into Battoes secured them with a number of Battoes & some prisoners & baggage." etc., etc. 3 pages, 4to.

16th.—Dated Albany, Sept. 21, 1777. Containing official information, and criticising the Resolves of Congress relative to duties of the Auditors of the Treasury. 2 pages, folio.

17th —Dated Albany, Oct. 4, 1777. A long and interesting letter speaking of the battle of Brandywine and Gen'l Washington's Victory, and detailing news of the battle between Burgoyne's and Gate's armies, in which the latter came off victorious; also mentions a little tiff between Gen'ls Arnold and Gates. "Genl Arnold was for going with a reinforcement which was overruled by the Commander in Chief & on the former urging it, the latter drew his Sword & said he Commanded & would be obeyed or something to that purpose & those Gentlemen are at advariance. * * My God are we to be sacrificed by Jealousie and party." 5 pages, 4to.

18th.—Dated Oct. 8, 1777. "Thanks to Providence in the midst of bad news, something good turns up, for in the night news came in from Camp of a battle in which we were successful. The Enemy began the attack at 4 O'clock both parties kept reinforcing, it lasted till dark, our people took a number of Prisoners, got possession of their flying camp 8 pieces of brass cannon, tents, baggage, &c with all their ontworks and encamped on the spot, amongst the prisoners, is a Carleton, Q. M. Genl, Sir F. Clarkson, Aid de Camp to Genl Burgoyne, & some other field officers I think 190 Prisoners, besides their wounded, Genl Arnold & Genl Lincoln wounded in the leg, the latter will be cut off, but hope of the former," etc. 1 page, 4to.

19th.—Dated Albany, Oct. 15, 1777. "A Thousand Men were ordered to March (from a body of men we had entrenched at Fort Edwards) down toward the Enemy, but on Monday Evening Genl Burgoyne sent a flagg to acquaint Genl Gates that if it was agreable, he would send out a field Officer to treat on something of great Importance to both Armies & proposed a cessation of Arms until last night, which was granted & I think his adjutant Genl came out with proposal in which he aver'd his orders for destroying Genl Schuylers houses & property to secure his retreat, acknowledged our superiority in numbers, & his inferiority & to prevent the further effusion of blood, thought it would be best to come to some term of accommodation. Genl Gates, as we hear sent him for answer, he had no other terms to give, than for them to surrender themselves prisoners of War, in which case the Officers should be allowed their baggage. Genl Burgoyne only objected to one article, that of grounding their Arms within works, & the matter was settled to allow them to march out with the honors of war & Ground their arms on Genl Schuylers Land. So Dear Sir I sincerely give you joy of the greatest Event that has ever happened America, of a Lieut Genl of the British Army Capitulating for himself & Army on the open field." 3 pages, 4to.

20th.—Dated Albany, Nov. 10, 1777. "I have received from Col Hazen a most particular narrative of every motion of Genl Washingtons Army, from the Day before the Battle of the Brandywine until after the affair at Germantown. * * * * * Genl Burgoyne after remaining here to days * * * * set off to Boston, I was really glad when he was gone, I expected immediately on the Surrender of that Army all the Continental Troops that could be spared, would have been hurried down, instead o' which they remain quietly & uselessly encamped here, however upon the requisition of Genl Washington, by Col Hamilton, Genl Gates, has sent down a reinforcement, (as I understand with great reluctance) to Genl Washington, * * * * I understand he and Gen Washington are not on the best of terms." 4to.

21st.—Dated Albany, Dec. 30, 1777. "Genl Gates has been ordered by Congress to Fish Kiln & in conjunction with Gov Clinton & 3 others to render the North River impracticable for the Enemy to pass, much time has elapsed & nothing done, his friends have wrote him to come down to Congress notwithstanding the Resolve, I suppose to Cabal, There are men base enough, as to wish to see & even would use their influence to put Genl Washington out of the Command." 4to.

22d.—Dated Albany, Jan. 16, 1778. "Suppose Genl Gates will now storm away against the commissioners &c." Folio.

23d —Dated Albany, Feb'y 3, 1778. On personal affairs. 4to.

24th.—Dated Albany, Feb'y 9, 1778. In reference to the expedition against Canada. "I fear the Northern Expedition will drop through, as the Green Mountain Boys are backward moving out, unless they have double pay, Plunder & Clothing for such as want, having the good of their Country much at heart." 4to.

25th.—Dated Albany, Feb'y 20, 1778. A particularly long and interesting letter in reference to the manner in which Gen'ls Gates and Arnold proceeded to block the expedition against Canada, as also all the details of the preparation for the expedition. "I am well convinced he (Gates) has not slept Night or Day, for thinking of means to prevent its taking place." * * * * "Gen'l Arnold was never easy, but when he had Genl Conway with him, and reading to him sheets of objections." "Genl Arnold although incapable of Service and only detained here on account of his misfortune, as he came up a kind of volunteer, has assumed the command issues orders, and receives returns, I dont think he would accept second in command in Heaven." This letter was forwarded by Col. Koscinszko. Folio, 4 pages.

26th.—Dated Albany, April 24, 1778. "We have had Alarm No 1, of 7 armed vessels having appeared at Ty & 6 or 700 Men (it is said) desembarking. * * * * Warner's Regiment has just been ordered down here, and this day marched for Bennington." Folio.

27th.—Dated Albany, May 26, 1778. "I will be bold to say, that one month's vigorous exertion of our abilities would free us from these daring Islanders, & drive them, where their declining State, has most need of their Service." 4to, 3 pages.

28th.—Dated Albany, June 2, 1778. Interesting letter giving a description of the way which Gen'l Gates ordered away his forces for the defence of Albany and its neighborhood, leaving the county exposed to the attacks of the Tories. 4to, 3 pages.

29th.—Dated Albany, June 27, 1778. On personal affairs. 4to.

30th.—Dated Albany, Aug. 7, 1778. "We are in hourly expectation to hear that Rhode Island is in our possession, and then for New York. O Rare George III, * * * I have no patience when I think this is giving people unlimited Power. There is a deal of difference, in the ideas of some people between discretionary and unlimited power, but with an honest thinking Man, they are the Same." Folio, 2 pages.

31st.—Dated Albany, Oct. 10, 1778. "It is reported here that the Commissioners have received unlimited orders to treat with us on any terms, I am for nothing without the concurrence of France, who have brought Britain to this state of condescention much against their inclination." 4to, 4 pages.

32d.—Dated Albany, Nov. 15, 1778. Long and interesting letter containing a detailed description of the burning of Schohary, the capture of the Fort. The massacre of the men, women and children in it by the Tories and Indians. 4to, 3 pages.
A forecast of this occurrence is given in letter 28.

33d.—Dated Albany, Dec. 20, 1778. A long letter referring to the massacre at Schohary and Cherry Valley, complaining of Washington's order removing Gen'l Hood from command, and commenting on the causes of the depreciation of our currency. Folio, 4 pages.

34th.—Dated Albany, Feb'y 15, 1779. A long letter referring to Arnold's blocking of the Canadian Expedition, and commenting on the gambling habits of the officers of the Army in his district. Folio, 2 pages.

35th.—Dated Albany. On Public Matters Folio, 3 pages.

98 Hand, Gen'l Edward, the Revolutionary Correspondence of, with Jas. Milligan, Commissioner of Accounts at Philadelphia, taking in the period from Aug. 5, 1776, to Oct. 10, 1784, containing interesting particulars relating to the Massacre at Schohary and Cherry Valley, as also, other news of interest ; in all, 8 letters. 4to.

99 Trumbull, Jonathan, Jr., Commissary Gen'l Revolutionary War. Autograph Letter, Signed. Dated Lebanon, 10th Month, 1780. 4to, 3 pages.

Interesting letter commenting upon the position offered him by Congress as Commissioner of the Treasury.

100 Original Autograph Application, Signed, of Benj. Mifflin for the Position as Commissioner of the Treasury. Signed also by Jno. Bayard, Jno. Nicholson, Jos. Howell, Jr., and Thos. Mifflin. Dated Philadelphia, March 23, 1784. Folio, 2 pages.

101 Warrant Signed by Robt. Morris, Treasurer of the United States, to the Comptroller of the Treasury, dated Oct. 5, 1784, instructing certain moneys to be paid to Michael Hillegas, together with the Autograph Receipt for the same of Michael Hillegas as Treasurer, with the Provisional Seal attached. 4to, 2 pages.

102 McKean, Thos. Autograph Letter, Signed as President of Congress. Dated Philadelphia, Oct. 16, 1781. 4to, 2 pages.

> The official communication to Jas. Milligan of his appointment as Comptroller of the Treasury.

103 McKean, Thos. Documents, Signed, as Chief Justice of Pennsylvania. Dated Yorktown, February 21, 1778, and October 25, 1781. 4to. 2 pieces.

> Certifying that Jas. Milligan has taken the oath of allegiance to the U. S.

104 Hancock, Jno. Signer to the Declaration of Independence, and President of Congress. Document Signed. Dated Philadelphia, August 16th, 1776, together with Fine Signature on Franked Address. Folio. 2 pieces.

> The Commission of Jas. Milligan, appointing him Commissioner to Liquidate the Accounts of the Army in the Northern Department.

105 Surrender of Burgoyne. The Commission of James Milligan for settling the Accounts of the Convention Troops. Dated Philadelphia, June 23d, 1779. Signed by James Duane, Elbridge Gerry, Wm. Carmichael and C. Griffin, Superintendents of the Treasury. Folio. 2 pages.

106 Thomson, Chas. Secretary of Congress. Autograph Letter, Signed. Dated New York, March 25th, 1785. To Jas. Milligan, with Signature on Franked address. Folio.

107 Thomson, Chas. Secretary of Congress. Autograph Document, Signed. Dated November 3d, 1778. Folio.

> Extract from the Minutes of Congress, wherein Jonathan Trumbull, Jr., was elected Comptroller of the Treasury, Jno. Gibson, Auditor, Michael Hillegas, Treasurer, and James Milligan and others Commissioners of the Chamber of Accounts.

108 Thomson, Chas., Secretary of Congress. Autograph Document, signed. Dated Oct. 23, 1779. Folio.

> Resolution of Congress electing Jas. Milligan Auditor-General of the Treasury.

109 Romans, Capt. Bernard, Author of the "History of Florida." Autograph Letter, signed, dated New Haven, Oct. 19, 1778, together with Receipt signed by Col. J. G. Dircks. Folio.

110 Penn, Jno., Governor of Penna. **Document signed.**
Dated Phila., Feb. 27, 1775. 4to.

111 Grant and his Staff. **Autograph of Major-Gen'l U. S. Grant, and all the Officers of his Staff, on one sheet of paper.** 8vo.

Neatly framed and glazed.

112 The Military Commission which Tried the Conspirators for the Assassination of Abraham Lincoln. Autographs of the members of the Commission, as well as the Autograph of Abraham Lincoln, and Reverdy Johnson who defended Mr. Surratt.

Neatly framed, glazed and lettered.

113 Generals of the Union Army. **Autographs of many of the prominent Union Generals, including Phil. H. Sheridan, Winfield Scott Hancock, Jos. Hooker, Jno. A. Logan, Jno. Pope, C. C. Auger, W. T. Sherman, Benj. F. Butler, Robt. Anderson, and in all 26 autographs.**

Neatly framed, glazed and lettered.

114 Autographs of the War Governors of the Union States. In all, 7 autographs.

Neatly framed and glazed.

115 Autograph Letter of Gen'l W. T. Sherman, and Autographs of the Confederate Gen'ls, Robt. E. Lee and Fitzhugh Lee, and President Andrew Johnson.

Neatly framed and glazed.

116 Arnold Treason. **Copy in the Handwriting of Gen'l Robt. H. Harrison of the famous Anonymous Letter written by Gen'l Benedict Arnold, under the *nom de plume* of "Gustavus," to Mr. Jno. Anderson [Major Andre], of New York, dated Aug. 30, 1780, together with an Autograph Letter signed by Gen'l Robt. H. Harrison, describing how Gen'l Washington came in possession of the Letter, and the reason he made this copy.** Dated Oct. 17, 1780. Folio.

As this is the only extant copy of this letter in existence (the original has been lost or destroyed) we deem it important to quote its full contents

"August 30th 1780.

"Sir

"On the 24th Inst. I had the Honor to write you without date in answer to mine of the 7th Inst. received from your house of the 24th July in answer to mine of the 15th, with a note from Mr B—— of the 30th July, with an extract of a letter from Mr J Osborn of the 24th, I have paid particular attention to the contents of the several letters, had they arrived earlier, you should have had my answer sooner, a variety of circumstances has prevented my writing you before, I expect to do it very fully in a few days and to procure you an interview with Mr. M——e when you will be able to settle your commercial plan, I hope agreeable to all parties, Mr. M——e assures me that he is still of opinion that his first proposal is by no means unreasonable and makes no doubt when he has a conference with you that you will close with it. He expects when you meet that you will be fully authorized from your house, that the risques, and profit of the co-partnership may be fully and clearly understood

"A speculation might at this time be easily made to some advantage with *ready money*, but there is not the quantity of goods *at Market*, which your partner seems to suppose, and the number of speculators, below I think will be against your making an immediate purchase, I apprehend goods will be in greater plenty and much cheaper in the course of the season, both dry and wet are much wanted and in demand at this juncture, some quantities are expected in this part of the Country soon

"Mr M——e flatters himself that in the course of Ten days he will have the pleasure of seeing you, He requests me to advise you that he has ordered a draft on you in favor of our mutual friend S——y for £300— which you will charge on acco't of the tobacco

"I am in behalf of Mr M——e and C——d
"Sir
"Your most obet hum Serv't
"Gustavus
"Mr Jno Anderson
"Merchant
"In the Care of James Osborn to be left at the Rev Mr Odells
"New York."

"I hereby certify that the within is a true Copy of a Letter in the possession of His Excellency Genl Washington, in a hand writing evidently disguised, That this Letter was transmitted him by Brig Genl Parsons the 1st of October Instant, who then said it was from General Arnold and by a subsequent Letter that it was delivered by him on the 30th of August to a person who had obtained permission from him to go into New York, who suspecting it might contain something illicit, from the extraordinary precaution used by Mr Arnold with respect to it when he gave it, did not deliver it in New York, but after his return put it into his (General Parsons) hands on the 10th of Sept; that it should have been forwarded earlier to His Excellency, but supposing it to refer merely to commerce. He chose rather to make it a subject of private conversation than of a Letter, and that on his arrival His Excellency was just leaving Camp (alluding to his visit to meet their Excellencies the Count de Rochambeau & The Chevalier de Jornay at Hartford) so that it was left to the ripening of the horrid event to detect the unsuspected Instrument.

"The copy of the within Letter was requested by Col. Varrick & is given him by permission of the Commander in Chief.
"ROBT H HARRISON, *Secy*."
"Oct. 17, 1780."

☞ This copy of Arnold's letter was found amongst Gen'l Washington's papers, and is undoubtedly its first appearance in print.

The Noted Correspondence of Washington with Robert Morris on Important War Matters.

117 Washington, Geo. Autograph Letter, Signed, to Hon. Rob't Morris, with Signature on Franked Address. Folio.

Morris Town Jan. 13 1777

Dear Sir

If amidst a multiplicity of important matters, you could suffer a trivial one to intrude, I should thank you most heartily, for taking a letter or two of mine, when you do your own, by the Southern Mail, and forwarding of them, as opportunity offers, to the Camp. I have long since drop'd all private correspondence with my friends in Virginia, finding it incompatible with my public business. A Letter or two from my Family, are regularly sent by the Post, but very irregularly received, which is rather mortifying, as it deprives me of the consolation of hearing from home, on domestic matters.

I beg you'll excuse this freedom and do me the justice to believe, that with very sincere esteem and regard

I am,

Dr Sir Yr Most Obed. Ser
GEO WASHINGTON

118 Washington, Geo. Autograph Letter, Signed, to Hon. Robt Morris. Folio, 2 pages.

Morris Town, Jan 19. 1777.

Dear Sir

Your favor of the 14th, with the despatches from Congress, came safe to hand, and those for the eastward forwarded on I am thankful to you for the information of Capt'n Bell. Intelligence of the same nature had come to me before, and I had no doubt of the diversion intended to be made by Gen'l Heath towards New York, does not withdraw from the Jerseys, or detain part of the Troops said to be remanded from Rhode Island) but that a Storm will burst soon, somewhere How well we are prepared for it, my Letter to Congress, enclosed, will inform you.

I do immagine that the aim will be at this Army Our numbers will be estimated larger than they really are Gen'l Howe will not therefore, I should think, move forward, or leave us in his rear, but clear I am in my own judgment that he will indeavor to disperse this army, or move on to Philadelphia, unless his force is much less than we immagine, or he greatly misconceives ours, neither of which do I believe.

for this reason, I again beg leave to give it as my opinion, that no part of the Public Stores that can be dispensed with should remain in Philadelphia, and to request you, to urge Colonel Flowers, not to continue the operations of his department a moment longer than he can avoid in that place, as it is only intended, not to be idle, while he is preparing his Elaboratory &c &c at York, or Carlyle

With great esteem and regard I am

Dr [Sir]

Yr most [Obed.] Serv't

WASHINGTON

119 Washington, Geo.   Letter, Signed, to Hon. Rob't
     Morris. Folio, 2 pages.

Head Quarters Morristown, 5th Feb'y, 1777.
Dear Sir
    I have yours of the 31st ulto, and can readily excuse you not answering my letters with regularity, as I know the weight of important business that lays upon your hands.
    The Return of Stores made by Mr. Towers, is so small that I do not think the immediate removal of them any ways necessary. Besides they are such as will be chiefly taken up by the Troops upon their march, if there are any bulky Articles not likely to be wanted soon, they are better out of the way.
    Mr. Wallace wrote to Gen'l Sullivan concerning his plate, and have desired him to write to Gen. Heath, and know wether he has got it. You may depend that such steps shall be taken as will render strict justice to Mr. Wallace and the Public.
    I perfectly agree in sentiments with you, That it would be better for every suspicious person to be in New York, for which Reason you have liberty to send in Capt Jones in exchange for Capt Hallock, and Mr Palmer for Capt Dear, if there are any others, taken in merchantmen, that are not held as prisoners of War. Use your own discretion, only indeavor if you can to procure the liberty of Masters of Ships or other the same circumstances with themselves.
    I hope your ship will not loose her valuable cargo of Salt.
    I thank you for the copy of the King's Speech, which I think fairly bids the Parliament to prepare for an approaching storm, indeed France has done everything but make the much wished for declaration.
    I have given Mons Devolland a Lieutenancy in Colonel Patton's Regiment.
               I am Dear Sir
                   Sincerely and Affectionately
                        Yours
                           Geo Washington

120 Washington, Geo.   Autograph Letter, Signed, to Hon.
     Rob't Morris. Folio.

Morris Town Feby 12, 1777
Dear Sir
    I shall thank you for y'r care of the inclosed,—nothing of consequence since my last to Congress,—frequent skirmishes happen betw'n the Enemy's foraging Parties and our Scouts; but they come out so strong now, we can make nothing of them. Most sincerely I am,
                   Yr's,
                      Geo Washington

121 Washington, Geo.   Letter, Signed, to Hon. Rob't.
     Morris. Folio, 2 pages. (Written on his Birthday.)

Head Quarters Morris Town 22d Feby. 1777.
Dear Sir
    You are well acquainted with my opinion, upon the unexpediency of keeping any more stores in the City of Philadelphia, than are absolutely necessary for the equipment of the new Levies.
    I am at this time particularly anxious to have them removed. The enemy have lately been considerably reinforced in Jersey, and, from a variety of accounts are meditating some blow. I am firmly persuaded that they mean to attempt to reach Philadelphia again, as I do not know what other object they can have ultimately in view. They may first remove us from this, and our other posts, but they cannot remain at them for want of covering for their armory, which I imagine they will never again suffer to be cantoned over a great extent of country. I have certain information, that they have been projecting a portable Bridge to lay over the Delaware, and I do not see any great difficulty in transporting it from Brunswic to the Delaware, if they take advantage of the Roads being

hard and firm. The numbers, that are at present in Amboy and Brunswic, cannot long subsist there, and therefore adds strength to my opinion, that they are assembled there for some other purpose, than merely as a reinforcement.

The Salt that has lately been imported should be the first article secured.

Mr. Walton wrote me that he either had or was carrying it to a place of Security, but as I do not altogether depend upon his promises, I should be glad you would have an eye to that and the other matters in his department.

I know you have sufficient in your own, to engage your whole time and attention, but in times like these we must double our Exertions. I am Dear Sir

With the greatest Sincerity
Y'r most ob't Serv't
GEO WASHINGTON

122 Washington, Geo. Letter, Signed, to Hon. Rob't Morris. (Favor of Monsieur D'Armand.) Folio.

Head Quarters Morris Town May 19, 1777.

Dear Sir

Your favor by Monsieur Armand was duly handed me.

I have been happy to show him every mark of attention in my power, the considerations you mention, gave him a just claim to it,—and derived additional weight from your recommendation.

I am pleased to find Congress took such distinguishing notice of him, as they did in their late appointment, he has requested to have the command of a partisan corps, composed of Frenchmen ; to which proposal I readily assented, as I wished to avoid as much as possible making draughts from the corps already formed. I have recommended to him to engage as many as he can meet with fit for his purpose ; and have left it to him, to nominate such French officers, as he thinks qualified for the position to serve under him, as I confide in his making a judicious choice, I doubt not they will be such as I can approve.

He appears to me to be a modest, genteel, sensible young Gentleman, and I flatter myself his conduct will be such as to give us no reason to repent any civilities that may be shown him. I am with great respect

Dear Sir
Your most Obedient Servant
GEO WASHINGTON

123 Washington, Geo. Letter, Signed, to Hon. Rob't Morris. Folio, with addressed wrapper.

Head Quarters Morris Town, May 28th 1777.

Dear Sir

I transmit you the inclosed from General Lee which I have just received by a flag. The other inclosures, I beg may be immediately handed to the Gentlemen, for whom they are,— As I am this moment going off to the Camp at Boundbrook, I have only time to add, that I am with sentiments of real regard and respect

Sir
Your most obedient Servant,
GEO WASHINGTON

124 Washington, Geo. Autograph Letter, Signed, to Hon Rob't Morris. Folio, 6 pages, with addressed wrapper.

Morristown March 2nd 1777

Dear Sir

nothing would add more to my satisfaction than an unreserved correspondence with a Gentleman, of whose abilities and attachment to the cause we are contending to support, I entertain so high an opinion of as I do of yours——— Letters however, being liable to various accidents makes a communication of thoughts that way rather unsafe, but as this will be conveyed by a Gentleman on whom I can depend, I shall not scruple to disclose my mind—and Situation—more freely than I otherwise should do—

The reasons my good Sir which you assign for thinking Gen'l Howe cannot move forward with his Army are good, but not conclusive,—It is a descriptive Evidence of the difficulties he has to contend with, but no proof that they cannot be surmounted—It is a view of one side of the Picture, against which let me enumerate the advantages of the other, and see which preponderates.

Gen'l Howe cannot, by the best Intelligence I have been able to get, have less than 10,000 Men in the Jerseys and on board of the Transports at Amboy,—Ours does not exceed 4,000—His are well officerd, well disciplined, and well appointed- Ours raw Militia, badly officered, and ungovernable—His numbers cannot, in any short time be augmented—Ours must, very considerably (and by such Troops as we can have some reliance on) or the game is at an end.—His situation with respect to Horses & forage is bad, very bad I grant—but will it be better?—No—on the contrary, it is growing daily worse, and therefore an Inducement, if no other, to shift Quaters—Gen'l Howes Informants are too numerous, & well acquainted with all these circumstances to suffer him to remain ignorant of them, with what propriety then can he miss so favourable an opportunity of striking a capitol stroke against a city from whence we derive so many advantages, The success of which would give so much eclat to his Arms, and strike such a damp upon ours—Nor is his difficulty of moving so great as is immagined—all the heavy baggage of the Army—their Salt Provisions,—Flour-Stores—&c.—might go round by water, whilst by their superiority of numbers they might sweep the country round about of Horses, left by us.

In addition to all this, Gen'l Howes coming over to Brunswick himself—his bringing Troops which cannot be Quartered, & keeping them on Ship board at Amboy, with many other corroborating circumstances did induce me firmly to believe that he would move—and toward Philadelphia—and I candidly own, that I expected it would have taken place before the expiration of my Proclamation.—The longer it is delayed however, the better for us, and happy shall I be, if I am dissapointed.

My opinions upon these several matters are only known to those who have a right to be informed—as much as possible I have endeavoured to conceal them from every one else—and, that no hasty remove of the Public Stores at Philadelphia should take place (thereby communicating an alarm) it was, that I early recommended this measure, and have since urged it, well knowing that if it should be hastily set about when the Enemy were advancing, unfavourable impressions would be given & bad consequences follow. To deceive Congress, or you, through whose hands my Letters to them went, with false colouring, & unwarantable assurances, would, in my judgment be criminal, and make me responsible for consequences—I have endeavoured in my acts therefore to paint things as they really appeared to me, without adding to, or diminishing ought from the Picture.

I wish with all my heart that Congress had gratified Gen'l Lee, in his request—If not too late I wish they would do it still—I can see no possible evil that can result from it—Some good I think might—The request was *his* not the *Commissioners*, where then was the danger of hearing what *he* had to say; especially as he declared that it nearly concernd himself.

The resolve to put into close confinement Lt Col Campbell and the Hessian Field Officers, in order to retaliate Gen'l Lees punishment upon them, is, in my opinion, injudicious in every point of view, and must I conceive, have been entered into without due attention to Circumstances, & Consequences,—Does Congress know how much the Ballce of Prisoners is against us?—that the Enemy have near, if not quite 300 Officers of ours in their possession & we scarce Fifty of theirs? That Generals Thompson and Waterbury are subject to a recall?—Do they immagine that these Officers will not share the fate of Campbell, &c? or, posibly by receiving very different Treatment, mixed with artful insinuations, have their resentments roused to acts highly Injurious to our cause & yet It is much easier to raise than allay Resentment, I believe no one will deny,—To this may be added, that every artifice is now practising to instill into the Hessians (in Howes Army) an Idea of our cruelty to their Brethren with us,—that we are actually selling of them as slaves, will not the close confinement therefore of their principal officers be adduced as strong Evidence of this—the confinement will be proved to them—the cause will be concealed—In a word, Congress should be cautious in adopting Measures that cannot be carried in to Execution without drawing after them a train of consequences that may be destructive in their effects.—

To sum up the whole, common prudence dictates the necessity of duly attending to the Circumstances of both Armies before the style of a Conqueror is assumed by either—and sorry I am to add, that this does not appear to be the case with us,—nor is it in my power to make C——ss fully sensible of the real situation of our affairs, and that it is with difficulty (if I may use the expression) that I can by every means in my power keep the life and soul of this Army together—In short when they are at a distance they think it is but to say—Presto begone—and every thing is done—or in other words to resolve without considering, or seeming to have any conception, of the difficulties & perplexities attending those who are to carry those Resolves into effect.—Indeed Sir, your observations on our want of many principal characters in that respectable Senate, are but too well founded in truth—however our Cause is just & I hope Providence will aid us in the Support of it--

If the Resolves of Congress respecting Gen'l Lee strikes you in the same light it has done me I could wish you would signify as much to them as I really think they are fraught with much Evil—We knew that the meeting of a Com'ee of Congress and Lord Howe stopped the mouths of many disaffected People—I believe the same would happen in the present instance, for their will be enough to say, if the application is known & not complied with, that the Congress were determined to listen to nothing—but the other matter relative to the confinement of the officers, is what I am particularly concerned about, as I thing it will involve much more than Congress has an idea of—& will bring on repentance when it is too late if carried into execution—

I have wrote you a much larger Letter than I expected when I sat down to it; and yet if time would permit I could enlarge greatly on the subject of it—at present I shall beg pardon for taking up so much of your time and only assure you that I am most sincerely,

Dr Sir
Yr Most Obedt Ser
GEO WASHINGTON.

∗∗—This most famous of Washington's Letters has been quoted in full by Sparks in the writings of Washington. Vol. iv., page 338.

125. **Washington, Gen., Letter, Signed to Hon. Robert Morris.** Folio, delivered by General Greene.

Head Quarters Morris Town 15th March 1777.

Dear Sir

Give me leave to introduce to your attention Major Gen'l Greene, who obliges me by delivering this. He is a Gentleman of whose abilities I place the most entire confidence. Your acquaintance with him justifies me in this.

The danger of communication by Letter our present situation, and the indispensable necessity of Congress knowing it, have compelled me tho' I can ill spare so useful an officer at this time, to send him to Philadelphia.

His perfect knowledge of our strength and of my opinion enables him to give Congress the most satisfactory accounts they can desire.
I am
Dear Sir, Yr Most Ob Serv't.
GEO WASHINGTON.

126 Washington, Gen., Autograph Letter, Signed, to
Hon. Robt. Morris. Folio, 2 pages.

Valley-forge Feby 10th 1778

Dear Sir

Your favor of the 19th ulto by Col Armand came to my hands a few days ago—Rest assured my good Sir, that that Gent'n misconceives the matter exceedingly if he thinks my conduct towards him is influenced in the smallest degree by motives of resentment, arising from misrepresentation.

I have ever looked upon him as a spirited officer, and everything that was in my power to do for him (consistently with the great line of my duty) I have done; but the conduct which Congress unhappily adopted in the early part of this War by giving high rank to foreigners, who enjoyed little or none in their own country, & in many instances of equivocal character, has put it out of their power without convulsing the whole military system to employ these people now; for viewing rank relatively, the man who has been a Major for instance, in the French Service finding a Subaltern (there) a field officer in ours, extends his views at once to a Brigade, or at least to a Regiment—and where is either of them to be found? without displacing, or disgusting our own officers, whose pretensions would be injured by it, & whose natural interest in & attachment to the cause of their country, is more to be relied on than superior abilities in capricious foreigners, who are dissatisfied with any rank you can give them, while there is yet higher to attain.

With respect to the particular case of Col Armand, I have only to add, that if it was in my power to serve him, I would notwithstanding he was influenced to resign in a pet.—The Corps he commanded has long since been reduced to a mere handful of men (under 50) & you are sensible that it is not in my power to raise any new ones without the authority of Congress—

Mrs Washington who is now in Camp, desires me to offer her respectful compliments to Mrs Morris & yourself, to which be so good as to add those of

Dr Sir
Yr Most Obed Serv't
GEO WASHINGTON.

127 Washington, Geo. Letter, Signed, to Hon. Robert
Morris, with "Quaere" in Washington's Own Writing, and Fine Signature on Franked Address. Folio.

Head Quarters Valley Forge 27th April 1778

Dear Sir

I have your fav'r of the 22d ins't. I take the hint in the friendly light in which it was meant, and thank you for your attention to a matter of the utmost importance, I shall write to the Board of War, and, without mentioning names, let them know that there is not that activity and exertion in the Conductors of our Elaboratories, that the advanced season demands. Some allowance must be made, when you consider that our Works were removed the last Winter from Allen Town and Easton to Lebanon and Carlisle, and that it took some time to have them properly fitted for Business, but as that has been completed, there can be no excuse for not going on briskly now.

The management and direction, of the Elaboratories out of Camp, belongs entirely to the Board of War, and I cannot therefore with propriety send an Officer to Superintend them, but I have no doubt that the Board will immediately look into the matter, and give necessary orders upon my representation.

I am Dear Sir
Sincerely Yours
GEO WASHINGTON

Quaere, have you ever received a letter from me, in answer to yours by Col Armand?

128 Washington, Geo. Autograph Letter, Signed, to
Hon. Robert Morris, with fine signature on franked
address. Folio, 2 pages.

Valley forge May 25, 1778.

Dear Sir

Your favor of the 9th Inst informed me of the acceptable present which your friend Mr Governeur (of Curracoa) was pleased to intend for me, and for which he will, through you, accept my sincere thanks — these are also due to you my good Sir, for the kind Communication of the matter, and for the trouble you have had in ordering the Wine forward. —

I rejoice most sincerely with you, on the glorious change in our prospects —— Calmness and serenity, seems likely to succeed in some measure, those dark and tempestuous clouds which at times appeared ready to overwhelm us, — The game, wether well or ill played hitherto, seems now to be verging fast to a favourable issue, and cannot I think be lost, unless we throw it away by too much supineness on the one hand, or impetuosity on the other —— God forbid that either of these should happen at a time when we seem to be upon the point of reaping the fruits of our toil and labour, —— A stroke, & reverse, under such circumstances, would be doubly distressing ——

My best respects in which Mrs Washington joins, are offered to your Lady, & with sincere thanks for your kind wishes, I remain

Dr Sir
Yr Most Obed't Serv't
GEO WASHINGTON

129 Washington, Geo. Autograph Letter, Signed, to Hon.
Robert Morris and B. McClenachan, with fine signature
on franked address. Folio.

Head Qurs at Spring field, 20th June 1780.

Gent'n

I am honored with your favor of the 3rd and have received — in good order — the pipe of spirits you were pleased to present me with, —— for both permit me to offer my grateful thanks, and to assure you that, the value of the latter was greatly enhanced by the flattering sentiments contained in the former.

In a struggle like ours — perplexed with embarrassments — if it should be my fortune to conduct the Military helm in such a manner as to merit the approbation of good men and my suffering fellow Citizens it will be the primary happiness of my life because it is the first & great object of my wishes.

To you Gent'n I shall commit the charge of making a tender of my respects and thanks to the rest of the others — with much esteem & personal regard

I have the honor to be
Gent'n
Yr Most

130 Washington, Geo. Autograph Letter, Signed, to Hon.
Robt. Morris, with fine signature on franked address,
Folio.

Passaic Falls, 11th Oct. 1786.

Dear Sir

I am happy to inform you, that   for
your favor of the 28th   was
etter Mr Elliot had
who was immediately   of
Prisoners to signify the   make   but
be   by this time, either   or up

It will convey the   to contribute   consent
care of any Gentleman on whose behalf you   ourself, when I can

do it with propriety—on other terms I am convinced you w'd not ask it,—I am with complem'ts to Mrs Morris

                Dear Sir
                    Y'r Most Obed Serv't
                    GEO WASHINGTON.

131 **Washington, Geo. Autograph Letter, Signed, to Hon. Robt. Morris. Folio.**

Dear Sir.
    Knowing full well the multiplicity & importance of y'r business, it would give me more pain than pleasure if I thought your friendship or respect for me did, in the smallest degree, interfere with it,—at all times I shall be happy to see you, but wish it to be in your moments of leizure if any such you have—
    Mrs Washington, myself and family, will have the honor of dining with you in the way proposed, to-morrow—being Christmas day.
                I am Sincerely & affect'ly
Monday 24th   Yr's
  Dec'r [1781]   GEO WASHINGTON.
☞ See Facsimile.

Clay-Randolph Duel.

132 **Henry Clay's Autograph Challenge to John Randolph, of Roanoke, Demanding Personal Satisfaction on the "Field of Honor,"** together with John Randolph's Acceptance, and all the preliminary correspondence which passed between the seconds, Messrs. Tatnall and Jessup. 8vo and 4to. 11 pieces, viz.:

No. 1. Clay's Autograph Challenge to Randolph. 4to.

                            Washington 31 March 1826
Sir
    Your unprovoked attack on my character, in the Senate of the U. States, on yesterday, allows me no other alternative than that of demanding personal satisfaction. The necessity of any preliminary discussion or explanations being superceded by the notoriety and the indisputable exisistence of the injury to which I refer. My friend General Jessup, who will present you this note, is fully authorized by me forthwith to agree to the arrangement suited to the interview proposed.
The Honorable   I am
    John Randolph.   Your obedient Servant
                                      H. CLAY.

No. 2. Randolph's Autograph Acceptance of Clay's Challenge. 4to.

                      Kersands near the 7 Buildings
                            Saturday April 1st
Mr Randolph accepts the challenge of Mr. Clay, at the same time that he protests against the right of any minister of the *Executive Government* to hold him responsible for words spoken in debate as a Senator of Virginia in crimination of such minister, or of the Government, (Administration) under which he shall have taken office, however honourable the manner of his induction may have been. (*Here follows sixteen lines of argument which have been crossed off by Mr. Randolph, who adds in lieu thereof the following postscript*) Col. Tatnall of Georgia the bearer of this letter is authorized to arrange with General Jessup, the bearer of Mr Clay's challenge the terms of the meeting to which Mr Randolph is invited by that note.
To HENRY CLAY ESQ. *Secretary of State.*

No. 3. Clay's Note to Tatnall. Saturday, April 1. 8vo.
No. 4. Randolph's "   "   2 o'clock. 8vo.
No. 5.   "   "   Jessup.   "   April 1, 1826. 8vo.
No. 6. Memorandum between Tatnall and Jessup. Washington City, 2d April, 1826. 4 to, 2 pages.
No. 7. Tatnall's Letter to Jessup. April 3, 1826. 4to, 2 pages
No. 8. Jessup's   "   Tatnall.   "   6, 1826. 4to, 2 "
No. 9. Tatnall's   "   Jessup.   "   6, 1826. 4to, 2 "
No. 10. Jessup's   "   Tatnall.   "   7, 1826. 4to
No. 11. The Cartel for the Duel, viz: 4to, 2 pages.

"MEMORANDUM OF THE TERMS OF THE CONTEMPLATED MEETING BETWEEN MESSRS. RANDOLPH AND CLAY

THE WEAPONS shall be PISTOLS each party to have one. The Pistols to be of *smooth* bore
THE DISTANCE—shall be *Ten paces* or thirty feet
THE TIME OF MEETING, shall be *Saturday* April 8th 1826 at half past four O'clock. P. M—
THE PLACE OF MEETING shall be immediately out of the Dist of Columbia & the first private Spot after passing the Toll bridge, on the new Turnpike road leading from Alexandria
THE MANNER OF HOLDING THE PISTOLS, shall be perpendicularly up or down—the word *perpendicularly* to be understood in its strict and literal sense.
THE "WORD" shall be "*Are you ready*" "*Fire*" "*One*" "*Two*" "*Three*" "*Stop*" The pistols are not to be raised or dropped until the word "*Fire*" at the word "*Fire*" the parties may fire as quickly as either may please at the word "*Stop*", should either party not have fired he shall be deemed to *have lost his fire*
THE RIGHT OF GIVING THE WORD AND THE "CHOICE" OF "STANDS" shall be determined by lot, it being however, understood that he who wins the one shall be considered as losing the other
THE POSTURE OF EACH PARTY shall be such as the convenience of either may dictate
THE PERSON WHO SHALL BE PRESENT AT THE MEETING, shall be two friends & a Surgeon with each party

THOS. S. JESSUP,
EDWD F. TATTNALL.

Note. The place of meeting was subsequently to the above arrangement, altered, having in View the convenience of both parties. E. F. T"

133 **Objections to a Winter's Campaign in 1777**, evidently in the handwriting of Robert Morris, on two pages, 4to, wherein the difficulties of Attacking the British in Philadelphia by Crossing the Schuylkill on the Ice are fully portrayed, as well as the impossibility of Clothing and Feeding the Army, or instilling the proper spirit into the discontented Officers, etc.

A very interesting document.

Gen'l Washington's Will.

134 **Gen'l Geo. Washington's Will.** An Attested Copy, on Twenty-nine Pages, Twenty-eight of which bear the Signature of Gen'l Washington. To which is appended the Schedule of Property comprehended in the Will, on Twelve Pages, the last page of which bears Wash

ington's Signature. The Will is dated July 9, 1790, and the Schedule is dated Mount Vernon, July 9, 1799. 4to.

This most interesting lot of Washington relics is the attested copy from the original will, made under the supervision of Gen'l Washington, for the use of his executors. His signature will be found at the bottom of every page (with the exception of one) of the will, as also at the end of the schedule of property, where it is witnessed by A. Rawlins.

This is the only copy of the original will of Washington, signed by himself, extant. It was copied verbatim from the will, now on record at Fairfax Court House, which is all in the handwriting of the testator, and consequently this, his own copy, is next in importance to that valuable document.

It was found amongst the papers of Judge Bushrod Washington, who was the active executor of the estate of Gen'l Washington, and is in perfect order.

It will be well to bear in mind, that the original will, is not witnessed by anybody; but only attested to as being in the handwriting of Gen'l Washington. Mr. Rawlins' name does not appear on it at all, but on this copy Mr. Rawlins name appears as a witness to the General's signature, and the whole body of the document is in his handwriting.

The size of the paper and the quality of the paper (according to the statement of Mr. Forrest W. Brown, who discovered it amongst Bushrod Washington's papers) is the same as that used in the original will.

For proofs as to the authenticity of the will, see the Monograph which accompanies this Catalogue.

135 **Armand, General, Mrqs. de la Rouerie.** Autograph Letter, Signed, to Captain Baptiste Verdier. Folio.

York town pennselvania November 25th 1783

Sir

Receive here my acknowlegement of the activity, bravery & zeal with which you have served as a volunteer during the Campaign 1778 and as lieutenant since the beginning of the year 1780 in the first partisan legion under my command, your military conduct in that corps & during the time you was a lieutenant in General pulaski's legion would have made me anxious to see you promoted to the Command of a company if the war had continued & as you was the first lieutenant of the legion no doubt but your promotion would soon have taken place.

I shall in a few days give an account of your conduct to his Excellency Général Washington & request him to give it from under his hand that authenticity which it deserves.

My desire is that these lines may convey to the mind of whom it may concern a true idea of your merits & of the esteem & particular regard with which I have the honor to be

Your most obt hble st

ARMAND MQRS DE LA ROUERIE

General Armand was a prominent General in the Revolutionary War. In one of the Washington letters (this Catalogue), will be found mention of him as Colonel.

His *full* autograph letters in English are an extreme rarity.

Braddock's Expedition.

136 **The Original Minutes in the Handwriting of W. Shirley** (son of Gov. Shirley), Secretary to the Council held at camp, Alexandria, Virginia, April 14, 1755, in which the preliminaries of Gen'l Braddock's Expedition for the reduction of Fort Duquesne were officially arranged. On 3 pages, folio.

An unique and highly interesting document of the utmost historical importance

See fac-similes

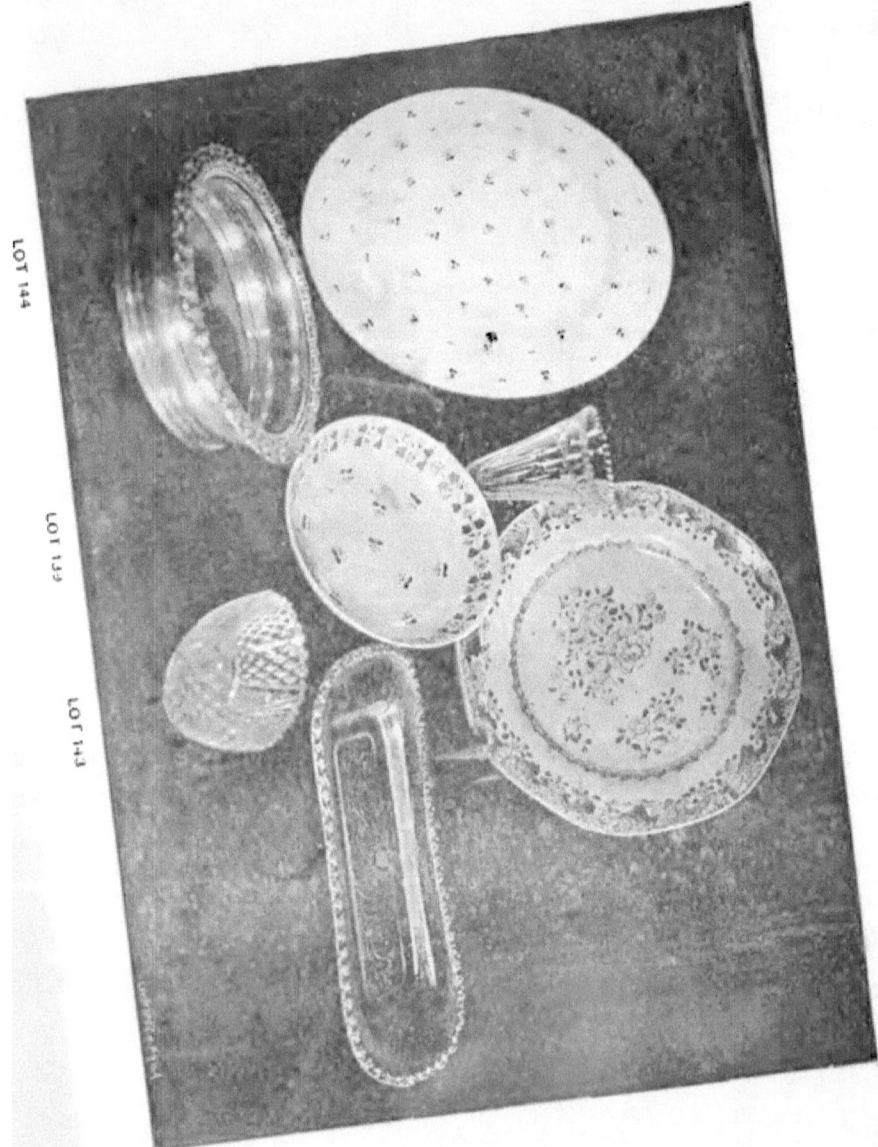

LOT 144

LOT 139

LOT 143

Relics of Gen'l Washington.

137 **Washington's Two Wine Coasters,** Silver Plated on Copper, of English manufacture, six inches in diameter.

 Washington only possessed four of these coasters, which were used on his table during his Presidency and afterwards at Mount Vernon. These two were inherited by Lawrence Lewis, his nephew, will be sold with the choice of one or both.
 Accompanied with certificate of authenticity from H. L. D. Lewis.

138 **Washington's Snuffer Tray,** Silver Plated on Copper, of English Manufacture. Oblong. Handsome design.

 Used by Gen'l Washington in sealing letters. Some of the wax still adheres to the edge. Inherited by Lawrence Lewis from the General's estate.
 Accompanied with certificate of authenticity from H. L. D. Lewis.

139 **Washington's Punch Glass.** Old English Rose Cut Glass, with handle.

 Used by Washington during his Presidency and afterwards at Mount Vernon. Inherited by Lawrence Lewis from the General's estate.
 Accompanied with certificate of authenticity from H. L. D. Lewis.

140 **Washington's Jelly or Wine Glass.** Old English Rose Cut Glass.

 Used by Washington during his Presidency and afterwards at Mount Vernon. Inherited by Lawrence Lewis from the General's Estate.
 Accompanied with certificate of authencity from H. L. D. Lewis.

141 **Washington's Salt Cellar.** Old English Rose Cut Glass. Oblong. Deep. Beautiful Pattern.

 Used by the General during his Presidency and afterwards at Mount Vernon. Inherited by Lawrence Lewis from the Washington estate.
 Accompanied with certificate of authenticity from H. L. D. Lewis.

142 **Another.** To match. Slightly Damaged.

143 **Washington's Plate.** Decorated Blue Canton China Dinner Plate. Octagonal. Diameter, 9 inches.

 Used by General Washington during his Presidency and afterwards at Mount Vernon, and one of the Set, the balance of which was purchased from the Lewis Family by the United States Government. Inherited by Lawrence Lewis from the Washington estate.
 Accompanied with certificate of authenticity from H. L. D. Lewis.

144 **Washington's Plate.** Decorated French China Tea Plates. Diameter, 8½ inches.

 Used by General Washington during his Presidency and afterwards at Mount

* Vernon, and one of the lot of Chinaware, the balance of which was purchased from the Lewis Family by the United States Government. Inherited by Lawrence Lewis from the General's estate.
Accompanied with certificate of authenticity from H. L. D. Lewis.

145 **Washington's Copy of the Engraving of the Battle of Bunker Hill and Death of Warren**, from the Original Painting by Jno. Trumbull, Esq. Engraved by J. G. Muller, London. Published March, 1798, by A. C. De Poggi, in the original Frame and Glazing.

146 **Washington's Copy of the Engraving of the Death of Montgomery**, from the original Painting by Jno. Trumbull, Esq., and Engraved by J. T. Clements, London. Published by A. C. De Poggi, in the original Frame and Glazing.

General Washington owned two copies of each of the above prints, and by his will bequeathed one set to Lawrence Lewis and the other to Bushrod Washington. Those owned by Bushrod Washington are very much damaged and worm-eaten. This set is in very fair condition, and what little damage they have suffered through time can be readily repaired. This is the pair inherited by Lawrence Lewis.
Accompanied with certificates of authenticity from H. L. D. Lewis.

147 **Washington's Cup and Saucers.** Decorated French China: very deep.

Used by the General during his Presidency and afterwards at Mount Vernon, and were reserved by the Family as relics, aside from the lot purchased by the Government. Inherited by Lawrence Lewis from the Washington estate.

147½ **Another Saucer, to match.**

148 **Nelly Custis' Needle-Book.** A neat little Needle-Book made by Nelly Custis, (the adopted Daughter of Genl. Washington.) The outside of each cover is inlaid with a piece of the silk dress worn by Martha Washington at the last inauguration of Genl. Washington. On the inside of one cover is a little mirror, neatly inlaid, and to the other cover is attached the needle cushion and pocket, size 5 x 3½ inches. A beautiful specimen of the handwork of the *First Daughter of Our Country*.

Accompanied with the certificate of its genuineness, from H. L. D. Lewis.

149 **Martha Washington's Slipper.** A Black Velvet Slipper, studded with spangles, with long pointed toe and neat little heel. Worn by Martha Washington on full-dress occasions, and probably one, of the pair, in which she danced at the Inauguration Ball.

This exceedingly interesting memento of Genl. Washington's Wife is accompanied with the certificate as to its genuineness from H. L. D. Lewis.

148½ **Relic of Nelly Custis.** Work Box, decorated with Transferred Prints on sides and top. The work of Nelly Custis, General Washington's adopted daughter.

LOT 151

150 **Painting by Nelly Custis.** An Engraved Portrait of Mary, Queen of Scots. Very artistically colored by Nelly Custis, (the adopted daughter of Genl. Washington). In the original frame and glazing.

A beautiful memento, accompanied with the certificate of genuineness from H. L. D. Lewis.

151 **Nelly Custis' Portrait of Gen. Taylor.** An exceedingly beautiful Painted Portrait of Zachary Taylor, in a Little Black Oval Frame, mounted with Gilt work. Presented by him to Nelly Custis. Size, $3\frac{1}{2}$ x $2\frac{3}{4}$.

In this little work of art is embodied probably the choicest relic of President Taylor, and Nelly Custis to be had. It portrays the General in full uniform (Bust), the face in full profile to the left, and is certainly (although not in the strict sense of the word, a miniature) a very elegant piece of artistic workmanship.
Accompanied by the certificate of genuineness from H. L. D. Lewis.

General Washington's Violin.

152 **General George Washington's Violin,** with name of maker inside. "Jacobus Stainer, in Absam prope Oenipontum 1675."

A remarkable fine-toned instrument, inherited by T. B. Washington in a direct line from Gen. Washington.
This is the same instrument that was sold in the Washington Relic sale, of last April. Some dispute arising with the buyer of the Washington Will, who also purchased this, we consented to take the will back if he would consent to relinquish his claim to the violin, which he very reluctantly concluded to do. Consequently its re-appearance in our catalogue, to be sold for the account of Thos. B. Washington

Provisional Congress Chairs.

153 **Antique Mahogany Arm Chair, Upholstered Seat and Back.** Covered with Tan Colored Leather.

One of the chairs used by the Provisional Congress at Philadelphia during the Revolutionary War, and formerly belonged to the late Mr. E. D. Ingraham, of Philadelphia. The pattern is well known, being straight back and arms and grooved legs. In excellent order. Of course the covering is not contemporary.

154 **Another.** Matches the above, with the exception of the covering, which is Maroon Leather.

Other Interesting Relics.

155 **Grand Duke Alexis.** China Pitcher and Basin used by the Grand Duke Alexis, of Russia, whilst sojourning in the United States. Decorated with the Imperial Crest, painted in colors.

156 **Prince of Wales.** The Jordan used by the Prince of Wales whilst sojourning in the United States. White French China. Decorated with the Royal Crest. Painted in colors.

157 **Prince of Wales.** The Hair Brush used by the Prince of Wales during his trip through the United States. Ivory Back, decorated with the Royal Crest.

158 **Prince of Wales.** Two Large Irish Linen Towels used by the Prince of Wales during his trip through the United States. Decorated with the Royal Crest.

159 **Prince of Wales.** Three Irish Linen Napkins used by the Prince of Wales during his trip through the United States. Decorated with the Royal Crest.

160 **Charles Dickens.** The Canton China Jordan made to perpetuate the memory of Chas. Dickens by order of Mr. E. D. Ingraham. Handsomely decorated in the wild artistic highly colored style of the Chinese, with the name Chas. Dickens burnt in on the bottom (the inside).

> Mr. E. D. Ingraham, who was one of the leading entertainers of Mr. Dickens during his visit to Philadelphia, became greatly incensed at the ingratitude of Mr. Dickens for writing the American Notes after having accepted the unbounded hospitalities of the American people. He caused this little memento to be made, in order that he might positively express each night and morning, in a practical way, his supreme contempt for a man capable of such ingratitude.

161 **Colonial Relic.** Large Ivory Winder, used by Dames of the Colonial Period for winding yarn or silk, with screw clasp attachment for fastening to table. It opens and shuts like an umbrella, only with the double action. The whole made of Ivory, and forming an exceedingly interesting relic.

The Earliest Philadelphia Receipt Book.

162 **John Cadwalader's Receipt Book**, from March 22, 1711, to May 4, 1724. Oblong small 4to. Contemporary binding.

> Contains 104 signatures, amongst which will be found that of Thos. Willing, Thos. Chalkley, Jos. Shippen, Chas. Read, Wm. Rawle, Jno. Yeates, Richard Wiling, Jas. Logan, David Ewing, Jas. Gordon, Abraham DePeyster, Francis Richardson, James Bingham, Thos. Griffiths, Benj. Goldney, Jno. Hunt, Clement Plumsted, John Boudenot, James

Breckenridge, Alex, Arbuthnott, Benj. Paschall, John Owen, Geo. Claypoole, Geo. McAll, Thos. Moskin, Jr., Israel Pemberton, Thos. Grame, Jonathan Evans, Samuel Powell and Geo. Fitzwater.

Many of the receipts in this book will form a connecting link for tracing up Early Philadelphia Biography and History. Some are exceedingly interesting, as they are signed when the men bearing the above-mentioned names were apprentices to other Philadelphians. It is probably the Earliest Receipt Book relating to Early Philadelphia in existence.

159*a* **Prince of Wales.** Cut Glass Goblet, with the Royal Crest engraved on side. Used by the Prince of Wales during his visit to this country.

159*b* **Prince of Wales.** Cut Glass Wine, with the Royal Crest engraved on side. Used by the Prince of Wales during his visit to this country.

159*c* **Prince of Wales.** Cut Glass Claret, with the Royal Crest engraved on side. Used by the Prince of Wales during his visit to this country.

159*d* **Prince of Wales.** The Illuminated Crest, on cardboard, which hung in his room during his visit to this country.

Bust of Henry Clay.

162¼ Carara Marble. Bust of Henry Clay, Life Size. A magnificent piece of sculpture, and a true likeness.

Irving's Life of Washington.

Large Paper Copy, in the Sheets, Extra Illustrated.

162⅞ Irving's Washington. The Life of George Washington. 5 vols. Royal 4to, extended to about 10 vols. New York, G. P. Putnam, 1859.

Large paper, of which only one hundred and ten copies were printed.

[And] **Tuckerman, Henry T.** The Character and Portraits of Washington. Royal 4to, cloth. New York, G. P. Putnam, 1859.

Large paper, of which only one hundred and fifty copies were printed.

The whole work will be sold as one lot, on account of its being unbound, and still in the sheets.

Independent of the one hundred and two proof plates which form a part of the original work, many of which are GENUINE ,UNLETTERED FIRST PROOFS, obtained direct from the publisher of the plates (selected from all the proof-plates, before they were delivered to Mr. Putnam), together with the fifty-two choice wood-cuts on India paper, of the vignettes and head- and tail-pieces, which adorn the work proper, this most desirable copy in the original sheets, unstitched and untrimmed, with extra titles, contains five hundred and forty-six inserted illustrations of the most choice description, comprising thirty-eight portraits of Washington, two hundred and seventy-eight portraits of his compeers and associates, two hundred and twenty-two views and maps, and thirty-eight autograph letters, notes and documents of men who distinguished themselves in the service of their country during the Revolution.

Besides the above, there are six original drawings by the celebrated artist, James Hamilton, depicting various places mentioned in the work, drawn expressly for this set. The rare set of outline drawings by F. O. C. Darley, illustrating various events during the Revolutionary War, and retouched photograph by Scheuesselle of the Reading of the Declaration of Independence. The inlaying of the many hundreds of engravings was executed by one of the most noted experts, and we can truthfully say that it is almost impossible to distinguish the many portraits and views from proofs, on account of their brilliancy of impression and the dexterous manner in which the inlayer has performed his task.

An ardent admirer of the character of General Washington, the owner of these volumes, spent the leisure of over thirty years on their *con amore* preparation. They are in the *finest state of preservation, perfect in every detail*, the *text* and *plates*, without any exception, pure and spotless from beginning to end.

At this period, when the spirit of *Extra Illustrating* has taken such a firm foothold in this country, this, the *work of all works* for an American to illustrate, should command particular attention ; especially when we take into consideration the rarity and great beauty of the edition, and the vast amount of material that appears in this same catalogue that could be used to the greatest advantage of still further extending these volumes. Although this set at present, if bound up, would make a *Monumental Copy of Irving's great masterpieces*.

1627/8—Continued.

List of Some of the Extra Plates.

38 Portraits of Washington.

Engraved by Wolff; Baker, No. 40. Engraved by P. R. M.; Baker, No. 65. Engraved by G. R. Hall; Baker, No. 90. Engraved by Illman & Pilbrow; Baker, No. 121. Engraved by A. B. Durand, N.A.; Baker, No. 123. Engraved by H. B. Hall; Baker, No. 149. Engraved by W. Gunston; Baker, No. 164. Engraved by Tisdale; Baker, No. 173. Engraved by J. S. Andrews; Baker, No. 177. Engraved by I. W. Baumann; Baker, No. 183. Engraved by D. Edwin; Baker, No. 210. Engraved by T. Illman, Baker, No. 260. Engraved by Geo. E. Perine; Baker, No. 303. Engraved by R. Soper; Baker, No. 335. Engraved by J. Thomson; Baker, No. 342. Photograph from the original portrait by Stuart. Colored Miniature Portrait, as a Colonel in British Army. Profile Photograph from the mask taken from his face. Totally unknown Portrait in Stipple. Washington and the Duché Letter. Proof. Pedigree of the Washington Family. Illuminated (in miniature). Crest of the Washington Family of Virginia. Illuminated. And a Genuine Washington Book Plate.

Set of Ten Engraved Outlined Drawings, by F. O. C. Darley, depicting various important events during the Revolutionary War. Very scarce. Suppressed.

Portraits

Of Lieutenant-General Ralph Abercrombie. Engraved by H. Meyer and Ridley. Of Major John André, engraved by J. K. Sherwin. Of Brigadier General Arnold. Of President John Adams, engraved by Houston. Of Captain Asgill. Of Fisher Ames, engraved by Edwin. Of Sir Jeffery Amherst, engraved by Walker. Of Frederick Lord Baltimore, engraved by J. Miller. Of Aaron Burr, engraved by J. A. O'Neill (India Proof). Of Lord Bute, engraved by W. Ridley. Of Admiral Boscawen, engraved by Ravenet. Of Sir Henry Clinton, engraved by Bartolozzi. (2d Proof.) The Same (1st or India proof). Of Lord Cornwallis. Of General Conway, engraved by R. Pollard. Of Myles Cooper, D. D., engraved by Dixon. Of General John Cadwallader (Private plate). Of Sir Henry Clinton, engraved by Cook. Of C. Cooley. Of Silas Deane, engraved by W. Angus. Of Colonel William Draper, K. B. Nabob (India proof). Of Rev. Jacob Duché, engraved by J. Charles Loan. Of Grant Dickinson, engraved by H. B. Hall and E. Wellmore. Of Oliver Ellsworth, engraved by P. Maverick. Of Benjamin Franklin, engraved by Cochin. First Edition, all letters on India paper. Of W. Hooper, engraved by Ingram. By W. Granger. Of Alexander Fraser, by J. Andrews (India proof). Of Major-General Nathaniel Greene. Very Rare. By Charles and James Scagn. Of Lord Hyde. Of Lord Howe. (2d Proof). Of Sir Erasmus Gower (India proof). Lord Geo. Germain. Of General Gates, engraved by Dupin. By Neagle, by Edwin. Mrs. John Hancock. Of Governor Hancock, engraved by W. Ridley. Of George Grenville, engraved by E. Harding. Of Commodore Hopkins. Of Gen. Montgomery. Bishop Thomas Burgess. Edmund Burke, engraved by Oxford. Of Lord Howe, engraved by J. Wessley. Of Of Lord Amherst (Proof, engraved by Angus). Of John Hancock, engraved by Angus. Of Patrick Henry. Of James Bowdoin by W. Ridley. Of Commodore Barney. Engraved by John Ve... (India proof). Of Admiral Arbuthnot, engraved by W. Ridley. Of Thomas Jefferson. Of Sir William Johnson, and of John Jay, engraved by H. B. E. (Proof). Of Commodore Jones, engraved by W. Ridley. Of James Hopwood and the Medallion Portrait. Of Ralph Izard. Of John by Leney. Of George King, engraved by Edwin. Of John Lowdon. Of Keppel, the Marquis de La Fayette. Major-General Charles Armstrong. Of United States Senators. Of S. T. Park Lord Anson engraved by Ed... Mezzotints. Of Count d'Estaing (proof), scarce. Of Lafayette. Original plate that was used. Of Lafayette, engraved by Dussaulx. Of James Clark Fiesinger. Of Henry Laurens, engraved by Dupin. Of French General, engraved by Kay. Of Pitt. Of Prince Ferdinand of Brunswick. Of Lord Londoun. Of Charles Lee. Of Lord La Trobe, engraved by ...

162⅜—Continued.

Reynolds (Proof). Of Marquis De Mont-Calm, engraved by J. Barbie. Of General D. Morgan, engraved by Edwin. Of Governor Morris, engraved by B. B. E. Of Hon. Robert Monckton, Governor of New York, engraved by Houston (Mezzotint). Major-General Wm. Moultrie, engraved by G. Fairman. Of Lord North, engraved by W. Ridley. Of General Putnam, engraved by T. Gimbrede. Of Paulding (Lithograph. Private plate). - Of Thomas Paine (Full length) and by Romney (India proof). Of William Pitt (French caricature). Of General Joseph Reed, engraved by J. Sartain. Mezzotint (Proof before letters). The Same (Artist proof). Of Count Rumford, engraved by T. Hooker. Of General Reed, engraved by Dupin. Of Madame Ruidesal, engraved by Buttre (India proof). Of Comte de Rochambeau, engraved by D. C. Hinman. Of Earl St. Vincent. Of Lord Sandwich (Mezzotint. Proof). Of Colonel St. Leger, engraved by P. Roberts. Of Hon. Lord Shuldham, engraved by Orme. Of Edward Shippen, engraved by Edwin. Of John, Earl of Sandwich, engraved by J. Corner. Of Sir John Sinclair, engraved by W. Skelton. Of Jared Sparks, engraved by S. A. Schoff (India proof). Of James Napper Tandy (Captain of the Liberty Artillery). Of Colonel Tarleton, engraved by C. Townley and by J. Walker, 1782. Of Charles Gravier, Graaff de Vergennes, engraved by Vinkeles. Of Hon. Edward Vernon, engraved by Harding. Of Richard Varick, engraved by J. Rogers (India proof). Of Major-General Wolfe, engraved by C. Spooner (Mezzotint). Of Bishop William White, engraved R. W. Dobson (India proof). Of Elkanah Watson, engraved by V. Balch. Of General Wayne, engraved by S. Harris. Of Colonel William Washington, engraved by J. B. Forrest and of Arthur Young, Secretary to the Board of Agriculture, engraved by W. Hinton and others.

Maps and Views.

Plan of the Position taken by Gen'l Burgoyne on the 10th of October, 1777; Engraved by G. Fairman. A Perspective View of the City of Quebec, the Capital of Canada, from the *Universal Magazine.* Sketch of the Action on the Height of Charleston, 17th of June, 1775, being the 1818 Reprint with the correction by Major-Gen'l H. Dearborn. An Exact Prospect of Charleston, the Metropolis of the Province of South Carolina, from the *London Magazine.* The East Prospect of the City of Philadelphia, in the Province of Pennsylvania, from the *London Magazine*, (1780). A Map of the Western Parts of the Colony of Virginia; Engraved by T. Gibson. Prise de Pensacola; Gravé par N. Ponce, Dessin par Lauson. John Malcolm, Tarred and Feathered by the People of Boston, January 25, 1774; Engraved by F. Godefroy. Journée de Lexington; Gravé par F. Godefroy. View of Quebec; Engraved by T. Dixon. A View of a Saw Mill and Block House upon Fort Anne Creek, the property of Gen'l Skeene, which, on Gen'l Burgoyne's Army advancing, was set Fire to by the Americans. View of the Taking of Quebec by the English Forces, commanded by Gen'l Wolfe, September 13, 1759. A Southwest view of the City of New York, in North America. A view of the Bay of Gaspe, in the Government of Quebec, situate in the Gulf of St. Lawrence, with a view of the House on the Beach in which Gen'l Wolfe resided in 1759. Plan of the Town and Fortifications of Montreal, or Ville Marie in Canada; from the *London Magazine*, 1760. View of Second Street, North from Market Street, with Christ Church; Engraved by M. Marigot. Philadelphia, von der Abend Seite, (rare old colored print of a view of the Schuylkill River, with the old bridge in the distance). Fort Ticonderoga on Lake Champlain; Drawn by H. Reinagle. Valley Forge; Engraved by Tiebout. View of East River or Sound, taken from Ricker's Island; Engraved by P. Maverick. View of Boston, from the Bay; Engraved by M. Marigot. A view of Quebec from Point Levy; Engraved by W. Knease. The Bloody Massacre, perpetrated in King Street, Boston, on March 5, 1770, by a party of the 29th Regiment; engraved, printed and sold by Paul Revere, Boston. Blank Card of Invitation to Dine with the President of the United States and Mrs. Washington. The Unfortunate Death of Major André at Headquarters in New York, October 2, 1780, and others.

162⅞—Continued.

Six Original Drawings

By the celebrated artist Hamilton. Washington's Family Vault. Head Quarters at Newburgh. Ticonderoga. Fort Putnam. Cowpens, and Fort Mifflin.

Photographs

Of the Reading of the Declaration of Independence before the Populace at the State House, Philadelphia, July 4, 1776. Retouched in India ink by Scheueselle, from which he made the large painting.

Autographs.

* **Koscuisko, Thaddeus.**
Portion of autograph letter signed.

* **Trumbull, Jno.** Autograph Letter, Signed. Hartford, May 27, 1778. Folio.

* **Trent, Wm.** Autograph Letter, Signed. Trenton, Lower Ferry, Nov. 9, 1782. 4to. 2 pages.

* **Rush, Benj.** Autograph Letter, Signed. Philadelphia, July 7, 1809. Together with autograph Poem composed by Wm. Rush, to his beloved mother in Canada, but copied on the third page of this letter by Benj. Rush. 4to. 3 pages.

* **Pickering, Timothy.** Autograph Letter, Signed. Philadelphia, May 10, 1799. 4to.

* **Peters, Richard.** Autograph Letter, Signed, War Office, April 19, 1777. To St. George Peale, Deputy Commissary General Military Stores, Baltimore, with postscript signed R. Peters, and signature on franked address. Folio.
On official business, in reference to military stores at Baltimore.

* **Ogden, Aaron.** Autograph Document, Signed. Aug. 28, 1797. 8vo.

* **Moultrie, Wm.** Autograph Document, Signed. Scrap.

* **Marshall, Jno.** Autograph Letter, Signed. Richmond, June 27, 1806. 4to. 2 pages.
In reference to the printing of his life of Washington.

1627/8—Continued.

* Morris, Robert. Autograph Letter, Signed. Jan. 25, 1804. 8vo.

    Invitation to Hon. Mr. Short to dine.

* Monroe, Jas. Autograph Letter, Signed. New York, Dec. 11, 1820. 4to.

* Madison, Jas. Autograph. Pasted on an Autograph Quotation by D(olly) P. Madison. Dec. 30, 1844. 8vo.

* Lear, Tobias. Autograph Letter, Signed. Department of War, January 30, 1815. 4to.

    Official business, to Isaac Shelby, Governor of Kentucky.

* King, Rufus. Letter, Signed. London, March 16, 1802. 4to.

    Referring to a case of Guns and Pistols, presented to "Our Government by the Bey of Tunis."

* Jefferson, Thos. Autograph Letter, Signed. Monticello, January 28, 1822. 4to, with signature on franked address.

* Jackson, Andrew. Autograph Letter, Signed. Washington, December 23, 1824. 4to.

* Johnson, Sir Wm. Autograph Letter, Signed. Johnston Hall, October 16, 1772. 4to.

    Interesting letter, referring to rascality of certain persons whom he employed to make a net for him.

* Irving, Washington. Autograph Letter, Signed. Sunnyside, October 5, 1858. 8vo.

* Hamilton, Alex. Autograph Letter, Signed. New York, September 10, 1790. 4to.

    Introducing Benj. Walker, (Aid-de-Camp to Gen'l Washington), to Wm. Short, Esq.

* Gates, Horatio. Autograph Letter, Signed. Rose Hill, July 30, 1798. 4to. 2 pages.

    Interesting letter to Mr. Jno. Mark, of Berkeley Co., Va., referring to the unwise course of declaring war against France, and giving good advice in regards to the duty of citizens voting.

* Everett, Edward. Autograph Letter, Signed. Everett House, February 29, 1856. 8vo.

1627/8—Continued.

* Boudinot, Elias, Autograph Letter, Signed, Burlington, Oct. 18, 1816. 4to.
  Interesting letter to Mr. Thos Sully, referring to his Portrait that Mr. Sully was painting.

* Burr, Aaron. Autograph Letter, Signed, New York, May 16, 1815. 4to, 2 pages.

* Arnold, Benedict. Autograph Letter, Signed, May 13, 1769. 4to.
  Addressed to "Dear Peggy," his wife.

* Ames, Fisher. Autograph Letter, Signed, Dedham, Nov. 13, 1807. 4to, 3 pages.

* Tarleton, Lieut.-Col. Autograph Letter, Signed in the third person; New Hotel, Feby. 22, N. D. 4to.

  Talleyrand, Chas. Maurice. Letter, Signed, Paris, Nov. 26, 1804. (In French.)

* Steuben, Baron. Autograph Letter, Signed, New York, Aug. 29, 1788. (In French.)
  Important letter relating to the capture at Yorktown.

* Lafayette, Gilbert Morte de. Autograph Letter, Signed, La Grange, June 15, 1830.

* Lafayette, Madame De. Autograph Letter, Signed. N. P. N. D. 4to.

* Howe, Richard, Lord. Letter, Signed, Dolphin, in Portsmouth Harbor, the 24th day of July, 1754. Folio.

* Carleton, Sir Guy. Autograph Letter, Signed, Montreal, 22d June, 1776. Folio.
  Important letter to Lord Barrington, requesting the removal of Lieut. Col Christie, on account of attempting to destroy that harmony and subordination so necessary for the King's Service."

* Clinton, Sir Henry. Letter, Signed, N. P. N. D. 4to.
  "Mr. W. Bayard having applied to me for permission to raise his Majesty's Letter, I am happy in bearing testimony that whilst I served in America, I ever found him under all his Loyalty and zeal for the King's Cause shown. That he frequently offered his services, requested authority to raise and to go with me into the Jersey. That he raised a regiment called the King's Orange Rangers, commanded by his son, Bayard, and that it has Commandant and his son Colonel Lt Col Bayard, was a Major."

162⅞—Continued.

* Cornwallis, Marquis of. Autograph Letter, Signed. Lower Grosvenor. March 16, 1795. 4to.

* Burke, Hon. Edmund. Autograph Letter, Signed. May 7, 1788. 4to.

* Burgoyne, Gen. John. Document Signed. Folio.
    Lieut. Jos. Mason Ormsby's Petition to the King, begging to be allowed to sell his commission as Lieutenant, in the King's own Regiment of Foot, and signed by J. Burgoyne, Colonel of the King's own Regiment.

* Amherst, Sir Jeffrey. Autograph Letter, Signed. St. James Square. 3d March, 1792. 4to.

* Fac-Simile Copy of Benedict Arnold's Commission as Major General in the Service of the United States. Oblong 4to.

Rare American Autographs.

163 Adams, Jno., Signer of the Declaration of Independence Document Signed. Washington, Feb'y 18, 1801. Also signed by Jno. Marshall, as Secretary of State. Folio.
   Signed as President of the U. S. on the pardon of Sam'l Springe, for counterfeiting bills of the Bank of the U. S.

164 Carroll, Charles, of Carrollton, Signer of the Declaration of Independence. Autograph letter, signed. Nov. 7, 1827. 4to.
   A fine specimen of his handwriting at the age of 90.

165 Franklin, Benj., Signer of the Declaration of Independence. Document signed twice. March 7, 1787. Folio, 2 pages.
   A petition to, as President of the Supreme Executive Council of the Commonwealth of Pennsylvania.

166 Huntington, Sam'l, Signer of the Declaration of Independence. Autograph letter, signed. Norwich, May 4, 1795. Folio.

167 Jefferson, Thos., Signer of the Declaration of Independence. Autograph letter, signed. Philadelphia, April 3, 1798. 4to.
   Signed also by Jno. O. Steele, Comptroller of the U. S.

168 Morris, Robert, Signer of the Declaration of Independence. Autograph letter, signed. Wt. Hills, Dec. 18, 1797. 8vo.

169 Paca, Wm., Signer of the Declaration of Independence. Document signed. (Partly written by him.) Sept. 6, 1791. 4to.
<small>Has signature also in the body of the document</small>

170 Rush, Benj., Signer of the Declaration of Independence. Autograph letter, signed. Philadelphia, March 5, 1813. 4to.

171 Boudinot, Elias, Member of the Old Congress and Commissary for the Exchange of Prisoners under General Washington. Autograph Letter, signed. Philadelphia, Jan. 23, 1792. Folio.

172 Coxe, Tench, Member of the Old Congress. Autograph Letter, signed. Nov. 13, 1789. 8vo.

173 Duer, Wm., Member of the Old Congress. Autograph Letter, signed. No place. No date. 4to. 3 pages.
<small>Rather an interesting personal letter on a Love Affair to his Friend Robert Livingstone, Jr., of New York.</small>

174 Fitzsimons, Thos., Member of the Old Congress. Autograph Letter, signed. No place. No date. 4to. 2 pages.

175 Ingersoll, Jared, Member of the Old Congress Autograph Letter, signed. Philadelphia, Jan. 21, 1809. 4to.
<small>Rather a Pert Epistle to Mr. Boudinot</small>

176 Jay, John, Member of the Old Congress. Autograph Letter, signed. New York, April 19, 1765. Folio. 4 pages.
<small>An exceedingly fine specimen</small>

177 Livingstone, Robt. R., Member of the Old Congress. Autograph Letter, signed. Clamont, Nov. 6, 1807. 4to.

178 Madison, James, Member of the Old Congress, President of the United States. Autograph Letter, signed. Montpelier, Jan. 19, 1822. 4to.

179 Monroe, James, Member of the Old Congress. Autograph Letter, signed. Washington, Aug. 5, 1814. 4to.

180 Muhlenberg, Frederick A., Member of the Old Congress. Autograph Letter, signed. In General Assembly, Dec. 14, 1780. Folio.

   As Speaker of the General Assembly, to President Joseph Reed, in reference to the issuing of Continental money.

181 Peters, Richard, Member of the Old Congress. Autograph Letter, signed. Dec. 19, 1811. 4to.

182 Symmes, John Cleves, Member of the Old Congress. Letter signed (partly written by him). Cincinnati, Dec. 20, 1795. Folio. 4 pages.

   From this letter and the above letter of Jared Ingersoll, (No. 175) Elias Boudinot seems to have been a very disagreeable person to deal with.

183 Yates, Peter W., Member of the Old Congress. Autograph Letter, signed. No place. No date. 4to.

184 Marbois, Barbe. Eminent French Statesman. Autograph Letter, signed (French). Paris, 1803. 4to.

185 Clay, Henry, Distinguished Statesman. Autograph Letter, signed. Ashland, July 21, 1843. 4to.

186 Clinton, Geo., General in the Revolution. Autograph Letter, signed. Washington, 1811. Folio. 2 pages.

187 Dayton, Elias. General in the Revolutionary War. Document, signed, (written by Jonathan Dayton), Elizabeth, May 11, 1795. 4to.

188 deHaas, J. P. General in the Revolutionary War. Document, signed Feb. 3, 1773. 4to.

189 Gates, Horatio. General in the Revolutionary War. Document, signed, Headquarters, Providence, May 12, 1779. 4to.

   Warrant to Pay $4,795.46, to Gabriel Allen, Paymaster to Col. John Topham's Regiment.

190 Hand, Edward. General in the Revolutionary War. Autograph, Letter, signed, Rockford, Oct. 12, 1801. 4to.

191 Heath, Wm. General in the Revolutionary War. Letter, signed, Headquarters, Boston Aug. 5, 1778. 4to.

    To " Major General Hancock." " I am just informed that you are determined to take an active part in the reduction of Rhode Island, and are to take the command of the Troops from this State,—Happy should I consider myself could I participate of the busy scenes, but since this honor must be denied me permit me to recommend Major Lyman, one of my Aids-de-Camp, to attend you on the Expedition."

192 Huntington, Jed. General in the Revolutionary War. Autograph Letter, signed, New London, Feb. 6, 1808. Folio.

193 Knox, Henry. General in the Revolutionary War. Letter, signed, War Department, Feb. 11, 1792. Folio.

194 Lafayette, Gilbert Motier de. General in the Revolutionary War. Autograph Letter, signed, Paris, Aug. 27, 1783. 4to.

Beautiful specimen.

195 Lincoln, Benjamin. General in the Revolutionary War. Autograph Letter, signed, Boston, May 18, 1790. 4to.

196 Moylan, Stephen. General in the Revolutionary War. Autograph Letter, signed, May 16, 1794.

197 Muhlenberg, Peter. General in the Revolutionary War. Letter, signed, Philadelphia, Oct. 13, 1801. 4to.

198 Putnam, Rufus. General in the Revolutionary War. Document, signed; signed also by Gen'l Wm. Heath. Folio. 2 pages.

    An Abstract of Pay for the Second Division of the Regiment of Foot, Commanded by Rufus Putnam, in the Service of the United States of America, January, 1777.

199 Pinckney, Charles Cotesworth. General in the Revolutionary Army. Autograph Letter, signed, Charleston, S. C., Sept. 26, 1817. 4to.

200 St. Clair, Arthur. General in the Revolutionary War. Autograph Letter, signed, Chestnut Ridge, Oct. 25, 1814. Folio.

201 Steuben, Baron. General in the Revolutionary War. Letter, signed, Feby. 22, 1784. 4to.

202 Stirling, Lord. General in the Revolutionary War. Document, signed, June 22, 1773. Folio.

203 Wayne, Anthony. General in the Revolutionary War. Autograph Letter, signed, Miamie Villages, Oct. 10, 1794. Folio.

204 Rochambeau, Connt De. General in the Revolutionary War. Letter, Signed, Paris, Jan. 7, 1784. 4to.

205 Blaine, Ephraim. (Great Grandfather of Jas. G. Blaine.) Document, signed, Philadelphia, Nov. 16, 1778. Folio.

206 Bloomfield, Joseph. Governor of New Jersey. Letter, signed, Philadelphia, Sept. 14, 1778. 4to. 2 pages.

207 Cadwalader, Lambert. Member of the Old Congress. Autograph Letter, signed, New York, May 16, 1789. 4to. 3 pages.

208 Dickinson, Philemon. Member of the Old Congress. Autograph Letter, signed, Nov. 15, 1798. 4to.

209 Hamilton, Alex. General in the Revolutionary Army. Letter, signed, Treasury Department, Aug. 14, 1793. 4to.

210 Lee, Henry. Member of the Old Congress. Autograph Letter, signed, Alexandria, Oct. 20, 1811. Folio.

211 Randolph, Edmund. Member of the Old Congress. Letter, signed, Department of State, March 19, 1795. 4to. 2 pages.

212 Lewis, Morgan, Governor of New York. Autograph Letter, signed. Albany, March 6, 1807. 4to.

Relative to the purchase of the two Reservations from the Cayuga tribe of Indians; also giving information that the Oneida Nation are willing to sell a portion of their reserved lands.

213 McLane, Allan. Collector of the District of Delaware. Autograph Letter, signed, Wilmington, Jan'y 12, 1808. 4to.

214 Pickering, Timothy, Secretary of State. Autograph Letter, signed, Department of State, Dec. 7, 1795. Folio.

215 Pinckney, Thomas. Autograph Letter, signed, Charleston, June 7, 1815. 4to, 2 pages.

216 Tallmadge, Benj. Autograph Letter, signed, Litchfield, Aug. 27, 1818. 4to.

217 Heyward, Thomas, Jr., Signer to the Declaration of Independence. Document, signed, Charleston, Sept. 9, 1788. Folio, inlaid, on Whatman's Paper.
On a warrant for Thomas Washington. Rare.

218 Rutledge, Edward, Signer to the Declaration of Independence. Document, signed, also by Thos. Knox Gordon, Chief Justice of South Carolina, Charleston, S. C., Sept. 21, 1773. Folio, inlaid, on Whatman's Paper.

219 Woodford, Wm. General in the Revolutionary War. Autograph Letter, signed with initials only, Camden, S. C., March 31, 1780. Folio, 3 pages.
An exceedingly interesting letter to Genl. Washington, from which we quote a few lines: "Col. Washington had a successful skirmish with an equal number of the enemies cavalry near Bacon's Bridge—he killed six and took seven, with the loss of one man killed and an officer missing,—he has taken a number of prisoners upon their lines, among them a Col. Hamilton, who commanded the North Carolina Loyalist, & was within a few minutes of taking Sir H. Clinton." * * * * * "By the enemies delay, they certainly have met with greater damage at sea than we know of—the loss is said to have fallen chiefly upon the Transports with their cavalry and heavy artillery—those at their batteries being taken from their ships."

220 McKean, Thos. Signer to the Declaration of Independence, Governor of Pennsylvania. Document, signed, Lancaster, Nov. 28, 1804. Folio.
On a license for keeping a public house.

221 Mifflin, Thos. General in the Revolutionary War, Signer of the Constitution, etc. Document, signed. Phila., Aug. 6, 1798. Folio.
Signed as "Governor of Pennsylvania," remitting a fine against Dennis Delany for keeping a tippling house.

222 Heath, Wm. General in the Revolutionary War. Autograph Letter, signed. Highlands, August 2, 1782. Folio.

223 Henry, Patrick. Member to the Old Congress. Eminent Statesman, etc. Document, signed, Council Chamber, December 17, 1784. Small 4to. Inlaid on Whatman's Paper.
On a voucher that Weedon Smith is entitled to the proportion of land allowed a private of the Continental Line.

224 Harrison, Benjamin. Signer to the Declaration of Independence. Document, signed. Council Chamber, June 30, 1784. Small 4to. Inlaid on Whatman's Paper.

On a voucher that Moses Williams is entitled to the proportion of land allowed a ... or of the State Navy.

225 Phillips, Wm. Second in command to General Burgoyne, and Captured at Saratoga. Letter, signed. Cambridge, June 17, 1778.

Interesting letter to Maj. Gen. Heath, in reference to the Convention Troops.

226 Ward, Artemas. General in the Revolutionary War. Document, signed. State of Massachusetts Bay, Council Chamber, February 4, 1777. 4to.

Signed also by Gen. Jno Whitcomb, Thos. Cushing, Sam'l Holten, and others, on an order on the Treasurer to pay a certain sum of money for Five Guns. Rare.

227 Reed, Jos. General of the Revolutionary War, Signer to the Constitution, etc. Document, signed. Philadelphia, July 24, 1780. Folio.

On a Decree of the Supreme Court to pay certain moneys to Randell Mitchell.

228 Wilkinson, James. General in the Revolutionary War. Autograph Letter, signed. No place. No date. 4to.

229 Grey, Sir Charles. British General. Document, signed, Maidstone, September 2, 1797. Folio, 2 pages.

Defeated Gen. Wayne at Paoli.

230 Weedon, Geo. General in the Revolutionary War. Autograph Letter, signed. Head-Quarters, Morris-Town, February 24, 1777. Folio.

An exceedingly interesting letter, from which we take the following: "I Send you by His Excellencies command, Col Duyckings of infamous Character. He was in the Service of the States, but on the Enemies coming into the Jersies he Swore allegiance to the King, took their protection, and went into Brunswick. He it is thought has been instrumental to many pieces of Intelligence gained by them. Notwithstanding his inimical conduct he has had the boldness to come amongst us since the publication of his excellencies Proclamation tho's refuses to avail himself of the Benefits resulting therefrom From the whole of his Conduct it appears his Business out, was more to gain a knowledge of our strength & Situation than any other motive, circumstances at present render it impossible to fix the matter on him as a spy. His excellency desires he may be taken proper care of in Your Goal till a future day."

231 Proctor, Thomas. Colonel of Artillery in the Revolutionary War. Autograph Letter, signed, Phila., Oct. 27, 1776.

231½ Angill, Israel. Colonel in the Revolutionary War. Document, signed. Folio.

    On Muster Roll of Capt. Allen's Company, Col. Israel Angill's Regiment of Rhode Island Troops in the service of the United States of America.

232 Boudinot, Elias. President of Continental Congress. Autograph Letter, signed, Elizabeth Town, March 8, 1784. Folio, 2 pages.

233 Hopkinson, Francis. Signer to the Declaration of Independence. Document, signed, (partly written by him). 4to.

For £1500.   In Council,
                          Philadelphia, May 12, 1779.
    Pay to Francis Hopkinson, Esquire, or his order, the sum of one thousand and five hundred pounds; for the use of the wife and children of the Reverend Jacob Duché, agreeably to the judgment of the Justices of the Supreme Court in that case given, He, the said Francis Hopkinson, having given bond to refund in case of claims upon the estate of the said Duché, as expressed in s'd bond,
    To David Rittenhouse, Esquire,   Jos. Reed,
                Treasurer.   President.

    May 24, 1779, received from David Rittenhouse, Esquire, Fifteen Hundred Pounds in full of the above order.
£1500.   Fra's Hopkinson.

234 Muhlenberg, Peter. General in the Revolutionary War. Autograph Letter, signed, Phila., March 9, 1804. 4to.

235 Hancock, John, Signer to the Declaration of Independence. Autograph Document, signed, Boston, April 2, 1791. 4to.

236 Fauquier, Frances, Colonial Governor of Virginia. Autograph Letter, signed, Williamsburgh, April 17, 1761. 4to, 2 pages.

Portraits of Gen. Washington.

237   **Houdon's Cast from General Washington's Face.** The plaster cast from the original mask taken by Houdon, the Sculptor, of Paris, from Gen. George Washington's Face.

> In 1785 Mr. Houdon visited this country to take a cast of General Washington's Face, for the purpose of making a Statue to his memory.
>
> This cast was taken from the mask by the Great Sculptor himself, and he presented it to General Washington. It was inherited by Lawrence Lewis, (Washington's nephew, and husband of Nelly Custis,) from the General's estate, and at the time Lawrence Lewis' son married the daughter of Dr. John Redman Coxe, Mr. Lewis presented the cast to the doctor. At the sale of the effects of Dr. Coxe, it was purchased by his daughter, Mrs. Sarah Coxe Boyer, the present owner.
>
> Although there are one or two copies of the cast in existence, still, this one possesses pre-eminent value, as it belonged to Washington.

238   **Original Portrait of Gen. Washington. By Rembrandt Peale.** A life-size portrait of General Washington, painted by Rembrandt Peale, for Col. Tilghman, of the Eastern Shore of Maryland, in 1818. It is a full bust in uniform. Head three-quarters to the left. Blue coat bordered with buckskin, with epaulettes. Buckskin vest, and white necktie. Oval, size, 2 feet by 2 feet 6 inches, in original Gold gilt frame.

> This is without question one of the strongest portraits of Peale, and certainly a most pleasing and said to a truer portrait of Washington, than those by Stuart.

239   **Lefort's Etched Portrait of Washington.** An Exquisitely Etched Portrait of Washington, by Henri Lefort, from the Celebrated Painting by Gilbert Stuart. Large oval. ARTIST'S REMARQUE PROOF, *Signed*, dated. Mounted on muslin.

> Excessively rare. A genuine proof. Dated 1881. A truly grand work of Art.

240   **Full Length Portrait of Washington.** A full length portrait, painted in oil. Size, 35 inches high, 24 inches wide.

> This is said to be the painting from which the line engraving by Heath was made. The head appears to have been painted by Gilbert Stuart, being remarkably well done, and with much detail. The figure and hands are carefully painted, while the details of the background are complete and accurate. The painting was cleaned in 1861, but needed no other attention at that time, nor does it now, being in excellent condition. It has been in the family of the present owner for the last sixty years, and is sold now to settle the estate.

LOT No. 238.

LOT 217

241 Full Length Portrait of Washington. A Copy in Oil of the Lansdowne Portrait, by Gilbert Stuart. Painted by Winstanley? Size, 48 inches x 30 inches, in Gilt Frame.

242 Oil Portrait of Washington. After Gilbert Stuart, by H. Watts. Life size. Gold Gilt Frame.

243 Oil Portrait of Martha Washington. By the same artist. A companion to the above.

The Rare Peale Lithograph.

244 Peale, Rembrandt. Large Head to the right. Life size. Drawn on stone by Rembrandt Peale. Lith. of Pendleton, 9 Wall Street Size of plate, including, margin, 16 x 22 inches.

   This copy (unique in this condition) of this excessively rare print, is the finest of the two known copies, the other one being in the possession of Mr. W. S. Baker, author of the "Engraved Portrait of Washington," and in very poor condition. Until within a very short period, this print was entirely unknown, and the famous lithograph (by the same artist) of the "Patriæ Pater" portrait, was considered to be the rarest, but subsequent investigation has dispelled that theory and established the fact that this is the portrait that Mr. Peale refers to in his communication to Wm. Dunlap, (Art of Design, Vol. II. page 57) "I was among the first artists who employed this admirable method of multiplying original drawings. My first attempt, in New York, was a head of Lord Byron and a female head from a work of Titian. In 1826, I went to Boston, and devoted myself for some time to lithographic studies, and executed a number of portraits and other subjects, and finally, a large drawing from my portrait of Washington, for which I obtained the silver medal from the Franklin Institute, at Philadelphia, in 1827. Unfortunately, the workmen, by some neglect, destroyed this drawing on the stone, when but a few impressions were taken."
   The opportunity of obtaining a copy of this print in this condition will probably never occur again. Collectors of Washington portraits should pay particular attention to this item.

245 Engraved Portrait of Washington, after Gilbert Stuart.
   This portrait is framed in the most exquisite style. The frame is oval at top and square at the base, lined with maroon velvet, upon which is arranged in artistic design in fire gilt of the American Eagle, surrounded with rays, accompanied on either side with olive branches. The whole inlaid, in the most magnificent style, with thousands of brilliants the color of rubies, diamonds, sapphires and emeralds. At the bottom is the name of "Washington," also set with brilliants. The above was on exhibition at the Centennial Exposition, and is a masterpiece of this class of work—must be seen to be appreciated.

246 After Gilbert Stuart, by E. S. Best. 8vo. Baker, 185.

247 After Gilbert Stuart, by E. A. Rice. India Proof before Letters. Folio, full margin. Baker, 310.

248 After Gilbert Stuart, by J. Chorley. Folio. Baker, 194.

249 After Gilbert Stuart, by A. H. Ritchie. Folio. Full margin. Baker, 312.

250 After Gilbert Stuart, by T. B. Welch. Folio. Full margin. Baker, 351.

251 After Gilbert Stuart, by Wright. 8vo. Baker, 356.

252 After Gilbert Stuart, by Perkins & Heath. 12mo. Baker, 304. Very rare.

253 After Gilbert Stuart, by Gimbrede. 8vo. Baker, 232.
This State is not described by Baker.

254 After Gilbert Stuart. Unknown. 8vo. Baker, 283.

255 After Gilbert Stuart. Unknown. 4to. Baker, 189.

256 After Gilbert Stuart, by Ballin. 8vo. Baker, 180.

257 After Gilbert Stuart, by Dupreel. 8vo. Baker, 205.

258 After Gilbert Stuart, by Edwin. 8vo. Baker, 210.

259 After Gilbert Stuart, by Goeffroy. 4to. Baker, 229.
With this is included the Portrait of Martha Washington. (Betty Washington Lewis) by the same Engraver.

260 After Gilbert Stuart, by Wm. Sartain. Large 4to. Baker, 326.
With this is included the Portrait of Martha Washington by the same Engraver.

261 After Gilbert Stuart. Unknown. 8vo. "A Paris, chez Menard & Desenne."

262 After Gilbert Stuart, by Marshall. Folio. Baker, 286. Proof before Letters. Framed and glazed.

263 After Gilbert Stuart. Wood-cut. Printed in colors. Rare. Framed and glazed.

264 After Savage, by Houston. 8vo, Baker, 130. Rare.

265 After Wright, by Holloway. 8vo, Baker, 87. Rare.

266 After Wright. Unknown. 8vo, Baker, 97. India proof.

267 After Wright. Unknown. 8vo, Baker, 86.

268 After C. W. Peale. Unknown. 4to. Full Margin. Baker, 16. Extremely rare.

269 After Rembrandt Peale, by H. B. Hall. 8vo, Baker, 381.

270 After Trumbull, by Sherwin. 8vo, Baker, 156.

271 After Trumbull, by Val. Greene. Large folio. Baker, 147. Framed and glazed. Very fine and rare.

272 Washington Family. Painted and Engraved by Savage. Oblong folio. Baker, 120. Rare. Framed and glazed.

273 Copy of the Same. Lithograph by A. L. Weise & Co. Framed and glazed.

274 Apotheosis of Washington. "Commemoration of Washington." Drawn and engraved by J. J. Barralet Stipple. Large folio. Very rare.

275 After Savage, by Walter. Published by C. N. Robinson, Philadelphia. Large folio. Mezzotint. Proof. "Patriæ Pater." Framed and glazed.
Baker, 183.

276 The Same. Published by C. N. Robinson. Printed by Goupil. Proof. Rare. Framed and glazed.

277 The Same. Published by Hugh A. McCann.

278 After Jno. Trumbull. Engraved by Warner. Large folio. Mezzotint. Smith, reprint.
Baker, 158.

280 After Stuart, by Cogniet. Engraved by Laugier. 1839. Large folio. Lane. India proof.
Baker, 417.

281 After Gabriel Stuart. Engraved by Jas. Heath. Large folio. Line. "Lansdowne Portrait." Published 1800. Brilliant impression.
Baker, 250.

282 After Stuart, by Rothermel. Engraved by A. H. Ritchie. Large folio. Mezzotint. Published by L. A. Elliot & Co., Boston.
Baker, 312.

283 After Stuart. Engraved by C. W. Carter. Large folio. Mezzotint.
Not in Baker.

284 After Trumbull. Engraved by T. Cheesman. Large folio. Stipple. Published by A. C. DePoggi, No. 91 New Bond Street, June, 1796. Very rare. Fine impression. Mounted on muslin.
Baker, 141.

285 After Stuart. Engraved by Illman & Pilbrow. Large folio. Mezzotint. "Tea Pot Portrait."
Baker, 261.

286 After Trumbull. Dessine par Couder. Engraved by Blanchard. Folio. Line. India proof.
Baker, 139.

287 After G. G. White. Engraved by Jno. C. McRae. "Father, I Cannot tell a Lie; I Cut the Tree." Large folio. Stipple.

288 Engraved by Jno. C. McRae. "The Courtship of Washington." Large folio. Stipple.

289 After Brueckner. Engraved by Jno. C. McRae. "The Prayer at Valley Forge." Large folio. Stipple.

290 After J. W. Ehninger. Engraved by G. R. Hall. "Washington's First Interview with his Wife." Large folio. Stipple.

291 After Robinson. Engraved by C. Tomkins. "The Provision Train." (Washington on Horseback). Large folio. Stipple. India proof.

292 After W. H. Powell. Engraved by Henry Cousins, "Washington's Last Interview with his Mother." Large folio. Mezzotint.

293 After Brueckner. Engraved by Jno. C. McRae. "First in Peace." Large folio. Stipple.

294 Drawn by F. O. C. Darley. Engraved by A. H. Ritchie. Triumph of Patriotism. Washington Entering New York, Nov. 25, 1783. Large folio. Stipple. India proof.

295 After Huntington. Engraved by A. H. Ritchie. "Lady Washington's Reception." Large folio. Stipple.

296 Drawn and Engraved by A. H. Ritchie. "Washington and his Generals." Large folio. Stipple.

Franklin Portraits.

297 From the Versailles Portrait, by Levy. 4to Line. Scarce.

298 From the Sumner Portrait, by Storm. 8vo. Line.

299 Combe's Physiological Chart, containing a Portrait of Franklin. Folio. Lithograph by Madley.

300 Sheet of Wood-Cut Portraits, containing a Portrait of Franklin. Folio.

301 From the Carmontel Portrait. Folio. Full margin. Line.
Brilliant impression of this rare portrait.

302 From the Martin Portrait, by E. Savage. Folio. Full margin. Mezzotint.
Restrike.

303 From the Martin Portrait, by Longacre. 8vo. Stipple.

304 From the Elmer Portrait, by T. Ryder. Folio. Line. Rare.

305 From the Elmer Portrait. 4to. Line.

306 From the Cochin Portrait, by St. Aubin. 4to. Full margin. Line. Scarce.

307 From the Cochin Portrait, by Rugendas. Folio. Mezzotint. Extremely rare.

308 From the Cochin Portrait, by Sprink. 8vo. Stipple. Rare.

309 From the Cochin Portrait, by Harrison. 8vo. Line. Rare.

310 From the Cochin Portrait. Unknown. 8vo. Line. Rare.

311 From the Chamberlain Portrait. 4to. Full margin. Line. Rare.

312 From the C. W. Peale Portrait, by Alix. Aquatint. Printed in colors. Folio. Rare.

313 From the Desreyes Portrait, by LeBeau. 8vo. Line. Rare.

314 From the Duplessis Portrait, by Janet. 8vo. Line.

315 From the Duplessis Portrait, by Bertonnier. 8vo. Line.

316 From the Duplessis Portrait, by Bertonnier. 8vo. Line. India proof, before letters.

317 From the Duplessis Portrait, by Bertonnier. 8vo. Line. India proof.

318 From the Duplessis Portrait, by Maurin. Folio. Full margin. Lithograph.

319 From the Duplessis Portrait, by Ridolf. Folio. Full margin. Lithograph.

320 From the Duplessis Portrait. Unknown. 8vo. Oval. Line.

321 From the Duplessis Portrait, by Delaistre. 8vo. Line.

322 From the Duplessis Portrait, by Chevillet. Folio. Full margin. Line. Scarce.

323 From the Duplessis Portrait. 8vo, Line. "A Paris chez, Menard & Desenne."

324 From the Duplessis Portrait. Large Folio Lithograph in Colors.

325 From the Duplessis Portrait. Unknown. Wood-cut. Large. Oval. 8vo.

326 From the Duplessis Portrait. Unknown. 8vo. Line.

327 From the Duplessis Portrait, Engraved by Bouvier. 8vo. Line. India proof.

328 From the Duplessis Portrait. Engraved by Bouvier. 8vo. Line.

329 From the Duplessis Portrait. Engraved by Pye. Folio. Full margin. Line. Scarce.

330 From the Bonneville Portrait, by Gautier. 8vo. Stipple.

331 From the Bonneville Portrait, by Ferdinand. 8vo. Line.

332 From the Bonneville Portrait, by Felicier. 8vo. Line. Scarce.

333 "Le Docteur Francklin Couronne par la Libertie." 4to. Aquatint. Rare.

334 Engraved by Krause. Folio. Line. Framed and glazed.

Miscellaneous Portraits.

335 Abraham Lincoln. Painted and Engraved by W. E. Marshall. Folio. Line. India proof, before letters. Framed and glazed.

336 Abraham Lincoln. Published by Wm. Pate, New York. Large folio. Stipple.

337 Death of Lincoln. Painted and Engraved by A. H. Ritchie. Large folio. Stipple. India proof.

338 Union. Painted by Matteson. Engraved by Sadd. Large folio. Mezzotint.

339 Ulysses S. Grant. Engraved by Dudensing. Large folio. Stipple.

340 Genl. U. S. Grant. Painted and Engraved by W. E. Marshall. Large folio. Line and Stipple. Proof.

341 Ulysses S. Grant. Published by J. C. Buttre. (Full length.) Large folio. Stipple.

342 Henry Clay. Painted by Nagle. Engraved by W. Warner. Large folio. Mezzotint. Original impression. Rare.

343 Wm. Penn. Painted by Inman. Engraved by Sartain. Large folio. Mezzotint. Original impression. Rare.

344 Wm. Henry Harrison, Painted by Hoit. Engraved by Pelton & Kemberly, 1841. Large folio. Line. Rare.

345 David Crockett. Painted by Osgood. Engraved by Childs & Lehman. Folio. Lithograph. Proof.

346 Charles Carroll, of Carrollton. Engraved by J. B. Longacre. 4to. Line. Proof. Rare.

347 N. Biddle. Painted by Sully. Engraved by Sam'l Cousins. 4to. Mezzotint. Exceedingly scarce.

348 Com. Stephen Decatur. Painted by Jarvis. Engraved by Henry Meyers. 4to. Stipple. Fine.

349 Com. Oliver H. Perry. Painted by Jarvis. Engraved by Henry Meyers. 4to. Stipple. Fine.

350 Capt. Isaac Hull. Painted by Gilbert Stuart. Engraved by T. W. Freeman, 1813. Folio. Mezzotint. Rare.

351 John Quincy Adams. Painted by Sully. Engraved by A. B. Durand. Folio. Line. Rare and fine.

352 Thos. J. Jackson, "Stonewall." Engraved by A. Varin. Large folio. Stipple. Proof.

353 Andrew Jackson. Painted by Sully. Engraved by Welsh. Large folio. Stipple. Proof.

354 James Monroe. Painted by C. B. King. Engraved by Goodman & Piggot. 1817. Large folio. Stipple. Rare.

355 Andrew Jackson. Painted by D. M. Carter. Engraved by A. H. Ritchie. Large folio. Mezzotint. India proof.

356 Andrew Jackson. Painted by Vanderlyn. Engraved by A. B. Durand. Large folio. Line. Rare. Framed and glazed.

357 Thomas Paine. Engraved by Krause. Folio. Line. Scarce. Framed and glazed.

358 Chas. James Fox. Painted by Sir Joshua Reynolds. Engraved by Williamson. 4to. Stipple. Framed and glazed.

359 Kemble in the character of Rolla. Painted by Sir Thomas Lawrence. 8vo. Mezzotint. Rare.

360 George, Prince of Wales. Painted by Sir Joshua Reynolds. Engraved by S. W. Reynolds. 8vo. Mezzotint

361 Joseph Bonaparte. Painted by Gerard. Engraved by Pradier. 1813. Large folio. Line. Full margin. Proof. Fine and rare.

362 Napoleon a Sainte-Helene. Painted by Delaroche. Engraved by Lafosse. Large folio. Lithograph. Colored.

Lafayette.

363 From the Bounieu Portrait, by Vangelistie. Folio. Line. Rare.

364 From the Mme. Meyer Portrait, by Boudrau. 4to. Mixed. Rare.

365 Lafayette. Engraved by Pagni. 8vo. Line. Very rare.

366 Lafayette. Unknown. Medallion. 8vo. Line. Rare and fine.

367 Lafayette. Engraved by Anker Smith. 8vo. Line. Rare.

368 Lafayette. Engraved by Massard. 4to. Line.

369 Lafayette. Engraved by Maurier. Folio. Lithograph.

370 Lafayette. Twelve Miscellaneous Portraits and Carricatures.

American Statesmen.

371 Simon Bolivar. Engraved by St. Georgio. Folio. Stipple. Rare.

372 Elias Boudinot. Engraved by Durand. Folio. Line. Rare.

373 Gouveneur Morris. Engraved by B. B. E. 8vo. Line. Brown.

374 "Le Celebre Hancock, Fresident du Congres." 8vo. Line. Rare.

375 John Dickinson. Engraved by Prevost. 8vo. Line. Proof.

376 Wm. H. Drayton. Engraved by Prevost. 8vo. Line. Proof.

377 Adams, Jefferson, Hopkinson, Hancock, etc. Fourteen pieces.

378 Admiral Wm. Penn. Engraved by C. Turner. 8vo. Mezzotint. Rare.

379 Wm. Penn. Engraved by Smithers. 8vo. Stipple. Rare.

380 Wm. Penn. Two Portraits.

English Royalties.

381 King Charles the First. Engraved by Boydell. Large Folio. Mezzotint. Brilliant impression.

382 Queen Mary, the Second. Engraved by Jno. Smith. Folio. Mezzotint. Fine.

383 Queen Anne. Engraved by Van Gutcht. Folio. Line.

384 George II. Engraved by Houston. Folio. Mezzotint. Proof before all letters. Rare.

385 George III. and Queen Charlotte. Engraved by Fritzsch. Folio. Line. Scarce.

French Portraits.

386 Louis XV. Engraved by Simon. Folio. Mezzotint.

387 The Chevalier D'Eon. Engraved by Burke. Folio. Mezzotint. Scarce.

388 Duke of Orleans. Engraved by J. R. Smith, after Sir Joshua Reynolds. Large folio. Mezzotint. Fine and rare.

389 Napoleon. Engraved by Louvion. Folio. Line. Rare.

390 Napoleon. Louis Philippe and Talleyrand. Three Portraits.

391 Madame De Stael. Engraved by Laugier. Folio. Line. Brilliant impression.

English Portraits—Military and Naval.

392 Admiral Lord Rodney. Engraved by J. Watson. Folio. Mezzotint. Fine. Rare.

393 Admiral Charles Brown. Engraved by Faber. Folio. Mezzotint.

394 Admiral Saml. Barrington. Engraved by Earlom. Folio. Mezzotint. Fine impression.

395 Stringer Lawrence, Governor of Nova Scotia. Engraved by Ezikiel. Folio. Mezzotint.

396 Lord Amherst. Engraved by S. W. Reynolds. Folio. Mezzotint.

397 Admiral Lord Hood. Engraved by Fiesinger. Folio. Stipple.

398 George Pochin, English Officer in the Revolutionary War. Engraved by Dean. Folio. Mezzotint. Proof before letters. Extremely rare. Private plate.

399 Admiral Lord Hawke. Folio. Mezzotint. Proof before letters. Scarce.

400 Le Major Robert Roger. 8vo. Line. Rare.

401 Robert Rogers, Commandeur der Americaner. 8vo. Line. Rare.

402 Col. and Lady Acland. Engraved by S. W. Reynolds. 8vo. Mezzotint. India proofs.

403 Lord Cornwallis. Engraved by Osborne. Large 4to. Stipple. Scarce.

404 Lord Cornwallis. From the Hibernian Magazine. 8vo. Very rare.

405 Lord Cornwallis. Engraved by H. Myer. Folio. Stipple.

406 Lord Cornwallis. Engraved by Bartolozzi. 4to. Stipple. Fine. Scarce.

407 Lord Cornwallis. Engraved by Chapman. 12mo. Stipple.

408 Major Andre. Engraved by Cooke. Folio. Line.

409 The Unfortunate Major Andre. 8vo. Line. Rare.

410 Sir Guy Carleton. Engraved by Rosenthal. Folio. Etching. Proof.

411 William Frend, Volunteer at Quebec. 8vo. Stipple. Private plate. Extremely rare.

412 Admiral Keppel. Engraved by Dupin. 8vo. Line. Scarce.

413 General Burgoyne and the Fair Virginian. 8vo. From *Hibernian Magazine*.

414 Col. Tarleton and the Amiable Miss Webb. 8vo. From *Hibernian Magazine*.

415 Sir Henry Clinton and Mrs. P—ll. 8vo. From *Hibernian Magazine*.

416 Gen'l Jas. Murray. Served under Wolf. 8vo. From *Hibernian Magazine*.

417 Barry St. Leger. Stipple. Extremely rare.

418 Admiral Sir Geo. Coburn. The Burner of Washington. 8vo. Stipple.

419 The Same.

420 Lord Howe. 8vo. Line. Rare.

421 Lord Howe, Gen'l Monckton, Lord Harrington, etc. 7 pieces.

American—Military and Naval.

422 Sir Wm. Howe. Engraved by Corbutt. Folio. Mezzotint. Contemporaneously colored by hand. Somewhat worm-eaten. Rare.

423 John Paul Jones. Engraved by J. E. Haid. Folio. Full margin. Mezzotint. Brilliant proof before letters.

424 Marquis De Montcalm. Engraved by Varin. 8vo. Line.

425 Alex. Lameth. Served at Yorktown. Engraved by Bonneville. 8vo. Line.

426 Gen'l Arnold, Commodore Hopkins, Gen'l Putnam and Gen'l Chas. Lee. Five contemporaneous Dutch portraits. 8vo. Line. Rare.

427 Benedict Arnold. Engraved by Prevost. 8vo. Line.

428 Benedict Arnold. After Du Simitier. 8vo. Line.

429 Commodore Hopkins, Gen'l Putnam, Gen'l Gates and Gen'l Lee. Engraved by Dupin. Four contemporaneous French portraits. 8vo. Line.

430 Gen'l Henry Lee, Gen'l Jno. Sullivan, Gen'l Geo. Clinton and Gen'l Philip Schuyler. Four portraits. 8vo. Line.

431 Count de Grasse. 8vo. Line. Rare. Contemporaneous Portrait.

432 Geo. Clinton, Vice-President of the U. S. 8vo. Line. Scarce. Old.

433 Com. Oliver H. Perry. Engraved by Gambrede. Folio. Stipple.

434 General Andrew Jackson. Engraved by A. B. Durand. Folio. Line. Framed and glazed. Fine impression.

435 General Thos. J. Jackson (Stonewall). Large folio. India proof. Contemporaneous. French equestrian portrait, by Goupel, of Paris. Framed and glazed.

436 General Robt. E. Lee, Companion Portrait. Framed and glazed.

437 General Robt. E. Lee. Engraved by Girardet. Folio. Stipple. Framed glazed.

438 General Robt. E. Lee. Engraved by A. B. Walter. Large folio. Mixed. Printed by the Lee Monument Association.

439 General U. S. Grant. Folio. Etching. Surrounded by French Text. Rare. On Japan paper.

440 Major Robert Anderson. Folio. Colored wood-cut.

441 Forty-four Religious Prints.

Legal Portraits.

442 Sir Saml. Romilly. Engraved by S. W. Reynolds, Jr. Folio. Mezzotint.

443 Henry, Lord Brougham. Engraved by H. Meyer. Folio. Mezzotint. Full margin. Fine and scarce.

444 Henry, Lord Brougham. Engraved by Shury. Folio. Mezzotint. Full margin.

445 Mr. Justice Haliburton. Folio. Lithograph. Scarce.

446 Sir Frederick Pollock. Engraved by Robinson. Folio. Line. India proof.

447 Sir Thomas Reeve. Engraved by D. Barron. Folio. Line.

448 Lord Chief Justice Rolle. Engraved by Hertock. Folio. Line. Proof.

449 Sir Sam'l Romilly. Engraved by Kennerley. Folio. Stipple.

450 Edward, Lord Littleton. Engraved by Robert White. Folio. Line.

451 Lord Camden. Folio. Stipple. Proof before letters. Rare.

452 Sir James Scarlett. Engraved by B. Holl. Folio. Stipple. India proof.

453 John, Baron Lyndhurst. Engraved by Chas. Phillips. 4to. Stipple.

454 Edward, Lord Thurlow. Engraved by Conde. 4to. Stipple.

455 John Paterson. Engraved by Thos. Watson. Folio. Mezzotint.

456 Hon. John Hyde. Engraved by Wm. Sharp. Large Folio. Line. Unfinished proof.

457 The Same. Brilliant impression. Full margin.

458 Sir Philip Francis, Lord Loughborough, Lord Erskine, Etc. 10 pieces.

459 Matthew Hale, Lord Kames, Lord Keeper Guilford, Etc. 8 pieces.

460 Thirty-one Natral History Plates.

461 135 Prints by American Engravers.

Indian Portraits.

462 The Seven Indian Kings, from South Carolina. Large Folio. Line. Exceedingly scarce.

463 Four Indian Kings. Engraved by J. Simon. Folio. Mezzotint. 4 pieces.
   Complete sets such as this, are extremely rare.

464 Three Engravings, American Aborigines.

Miscellaneous Portraits.

465 Pope Pius IX. Engraved by Metzmacher. Folio. Line. India proof.

466 Sir Jno. Suckling. Engraved by Geo. Vertue. Folio. Line. Fine impression.

467 Sir Isaac Newton. Engraved by J. Faber. Folio. Mezzotint. Extremely rare.

468 Warren Hastings. Engraved by Wm. Bromley. Folio. Line.

469 Sir Philip Francis. India Vindicated. Engraved by R. Pollard. Folio. Line.

470 Bishop Seabury. Engraved by Sharp. Folio. Line.

471 Chas. Wilson Peale. Engraved by Longacre. 8vo. Stipple. India proof. Rare.

472 Rev. Sam'l B. Wylie. Engraved by Longacre. 4to. Stipple. Scarce.

473 Benj. West. Engraved by Caroline Watson. 4to. Stipple. Rare.

474 Matthew Cary. Engraved by Thomson. 8vo. Stipple.

475 Edward Shippen, Martha Washington, Jacob Philadelphia, etc. 9 prints.

476 Benj. Lay. Engraved by Henry Dawkins. Folio. Line. Full margin.
The first copperplate portrait engraved in Philadelphia. Excessively rare.

477 Thomas McKean. Engraved by D. Edwin. Folio. Stipple. In brown.

478 Portraits. Sketches taken at a Print Sale. Engraved by Silvester Harding, 1798. Folio. Stipple. Very rare.

479 Louis XVI. Engraved by Bovi. 4to. Stipple. Printed in colors. Rare.

480 Mgr. Le Dauphin. Engraved by Bovi, pupil to Bartolozzi. 4to. Stipple. Full margin. Printed in colors. Rare.

481 Philip Syrg Physick, M. D., after Thomas Sully. 4to. Stipple. Private plate.

482 Captain Paul Jones. From an original drawing taken from the life on board the Serapis. 4to. Line. Rare.

483 Sarah Bache. Only legitimate child of Benjamin Franklin. Lithograph. 8vo. Only six copies printed, and stone destroyed.

484 Com. Robert Hopkins. From the Impartial History. 8vo.

485 John Paulding. One of the captors of Andre. Folio. Lithograph. Private plate. Rare.

486 Thaddeus Koscuisko. Engraved by Fiesinger. 4to. Stipple. Fine and rare.

487 General Lafayette. Engraved by Fairman. 8vo. Proof on India paper, before letters.

488 The Same. Brilliant Impression.

489 Captain Lawrence. Engraved by Williamson. 8vo. Stipple. Fine.

490 Richard Peters. Engraved by Gimbrede. 8vo. Stipple. Original impression. Rare.

491 Aaron Burr. Engraved by G. Parker. 12mo. Stipple.

492 General John Williams and General H. Dearborn. Engraved by St. Mermin. Two prints.

493 George III. Engraved by Volpato. Folio. Line. Brilliant impression.

494 General Lafayette and General Arnold. Engraved by H. B. Hall. Line and Stipple. 8vo. Proofs.

495 Sir Henry Clinton. Engraved by Cook. 8vo. Line.

496 William Clifton. Philadelphia Poet. Engraved by D. Edwin. 8vo. Stipple. Proof. Rare. Framed and glazed.

497 General Lafayette. Drawn on Stone by Rembrandt Peale. Lithographed by Pendleton, Boston, 1833. 8vo. Exceedingly scarce. Framed and glazed.

498 The Prince of Great Britain. (Infant George, Duke of Gloucester.) Engraved by J. Smith. Folio. Mezzotint. Framed and glazed.

499 Americ. Vespuccius. Engraved by Fairman & Columbus. Engraved by Maverick. 8vo. Stipple. Two portraits. Framed and glazed.

500 Frederick, William of Prussia. 4to. Mezzotint. Framed and glazed.

501 Genl. J. C. Fremont. Photograph from Life. Retouched in crayon by Edward Armstrong, from which he engraved the portrait. 8vo. Framed and glazed.

502 Henry Clay. Engraved by Jno. Sartain. Folio. Mezzotint. Framed and glazed.

Theatrical Portraits.

503 The Real Ellen Jewett. Folio. Colored lithograph. Published by Robinson, New York. 836.

504 Mrs. Peg Woffington. Engraved by Jos. McArdell. 4to. Mezzotint. Extremely rare.

505 Mr. Walker in the Character of Capt. Macheath. Engraved by J. Faber. Folio. Mezzotint. Rare.

506 Miss Phillips as Claudia in "Rienzi." Drawn on stone, by H. F. Dawe. Folio. Rare.

507 Mrs. Siddons on the Tragedy of the Grecian Daughter. Engraved by J. Caldwall. Folio. Etching. Restrike.

Rare View of Baltimore.

508 Baltimore in 1752. From a sketch then made by John Moule. Corrected by the late Daniel Bowley, from his certain recollection, and that of other aged persons. Engraved by T. S. Boqueta. Large folio Mezzotint. Full margin. Extremely rare. Fine copy.

☞ Eighty-one numbers were dropped here through mistake. The next number is 589.

Franklin Portraits.

589 Engraved by Angus. 1783. Bust. Head three-quarters to left. Circular in a rectangle. 8vo. Line. Very rare.

590 After the Duplesis Portrait. Engraved by Goldar. 1785. 8vo. Line. Rare.

591 After the Duplesis Portrait. Engraved by B. Andrews. 4to. Stipple.

592 After the Duplesis Portrait. "Franklin Citoyen des Etats-Unis." 8vo. Line. Rare.

593 After the Duplesis Portrait. Engraved by Delaistre. 8vo. Line.

594 After the Duplesis Portrait. Engraved by Scott. 8vo. Line.

595 After the Cochin Portrait. Engraved by Geo. E. Perine. 8vo. Mezzotint.

596 After the Cochin Portrait. Engraved by Smith. 8vo. Stipple.

597 After the Cochin Portrait. Engraved by Scoles. 8vo. Outline.

598 Engraved by J. A. O'Neill. 8vo. Mixed.

599 Engraved by Anderson. 8vo. Stipple.

600 Engraved by Scoles. 8vo. Line.

601 From the Martin Portrait. Engraved by Welch. 8vo. Stipple.

602 From the Martin Portrait. Engraved by Gobrecht. 4to. Stipple.

603 From the Martin Portrait. Engraved by Longacre. 8vo. Stipple.

604 From the Martin Portrait. Published by Milliette. 8vo. Stipple.

605 From the Martin Portrait. Engraved by Longacre 8vo. Stipple.

606 From the Martin Portrait. Engraved by Illman and Pilbrow. 8vo. Stipple.

607 From the Martin Portrait. Engraved by Longacre. 8vo. Stipple.

608 From the Martin Portrait. Engraved by Perkins and Heath. 8vo. Stipple.

609 From the Houdon Bust. Engraved by Allardin. 8vo. Stipple.

610 From the Houdon Bust. Engraved by Akin. 8vo. Stipple.

611 From the Houdon Bust. Engraved by Throop. 12mo. Line.

612 Engraved by Haines. 12mo. Stipple.

613 From the Martin Portrait. Engraved by Longacre. 12mo. Stipple.

614 Engraved by H. W. Smith. 8vo. Mezzotint.

Miscellaneous.

Birch's Views in Philadelphia.

615 New Lutheran Church on Fourth Street, Philadelphia. Colored. 4to. Original.

616 Second Street North from Market Street, Christ Church, Philadelphia. Colored. 4to. Original.

617 High Street, with the First Presbyterian Church, Philadelphia. Colored. 4to. Original.

618 Arch Street, with the Second Presbyterian Church, Philadelphia. Colored. 4to. Original.

619 Almshouse, on Spruce Street, Philadelphia. Colored. 4to. Original.

620 Gaol on Walnut Street, Philadelphia. Colored. 4to. Original.

621 State House, with a View of Chestnut Street, Philadelphia. Colored. 4to. Original.

622 Library and Surgeons' Hall, on Fifth Street, Philadelphia. Colored. 4to. Original.

623 High Street Market, Philadelphia. Colored. 4to. Original.

624 Bank of the United States, on Third Street, Philadelphia. Colored. 4to. Original.

625 Old Lutheran Church, on Fifth Street, Philadelphia. Colored. 4to. Original.

626 High Street, from Ninth Street, Philadelphia. Colored. 4to. Original.

627 South East Corner of Third and Market Streets, Philadelphia. Colored. 4to. Original.

628 Congress Hall and New Theatre, on Chestnut Street, Philadelphia. Colored. 4to. Original.

629 Back of the State House, Philadelphia. Colored. 4to. Original.

630 An Unfinished House on Chestnut Street, Philadelphia. Colored. 4to. Original.

631 State House Garden, Philadelphia. Colored. 4to. Original.

632 Pennsylvania Hospital, on Pine Street, Philadelphia. Colored. 4to. Original.

633 View on Third Street from Spruce Street, Philadelphia. Colored. 4to. Original.

634 The Porcupine Inn Yard, Rushmore Hill. Etched upon the spot by W. Birch. Colored. Small.

An unique engraving by the famous Birch; is one of his earliest works and was engraved before he came to this country. Highly important to complete a set of Birch's prints.

635 Schuylkill Bridge and High Street, Philadelphia. By W. Birch. 4to.

636 The Schuylkill Permanent Bridge, High Street, Philadelphia. Engraved by W. P. Farrand. 4to.

637 Death of General Montgomery. After the Painting by Trumbull. Engraved J. F. Clements. London. Published 1798. Large folio. Line. Open letter proof.

638 The Death of General Wolf. Painted by West. Engraved by Theo. Falckeysen. Large folio. Line. Open letter proof.

639 An East View of Grays' Ferry on the River Schuylkill. By J. T.(renchard). From the *Columbian Magazine*. Oblong. 4to. Rare.

640 The Desperate Fight of Capt. Pearson, of the "Serapis," and Paul Jones, Commander of the "Bon Homme Richard." Painted by Richard Paton. Engraved by Daniel Lerpinière. Proof. With portrait and autograph of Paul Jones inlaid in the mat that surrounds the print. Framed and glazed.

Excessively rare.

641 George III, The Apotheosis of. Engraved by T. Dixon. 1774. Mezzotint. Large folio. Proof before letters.

Very brilliant impression of this extremely rare allegorical print.

642 The Tea Tax Tempest, or the Anglo-American Revolution. Engraved 1778. Line. Large 4to. Rare.

643 Battle of New Orleans, and Death of Major General Packenham. Engraved by J. Yeager. Large 4to. Stipple. Rare.

644 William Penn's Treaty with the Indians, when he founded the province of Pennsylvania in North America, 1681. After West by John Hall. Large folio. Line. Rare.

Published by Jno. Boydell, 1775.

645 Libby Prison, Richmond, Va. Officers of the United States Army and Navy. Prisoners of War at Large folio. Designed and executed with a pen in Libby Prison by Capt. Robt. J. Fisher, 17th Reg. Mo. Vol. Inf. Lithographed by Ehrgott, Cincinnati, 1864. Large folio.

646 Bethlehem. View of one of the Bethlehem's principal settlements in Pennsylvania, North America. Engraved by J. Noual, London. Stipple. In colors. Folio. Rare.

647 Quebec, View of the Taking of. Sept. 13, 1759. Folio.

Extremely rare contemporaneous print. Colored by hand.

648 **Paul Revere. Boston Massacre Engraving.** The Bloody Massacre perpetrated in King Street, Boston, March 5, 1770, by a party of soldiers. Engraved, printed and sold by Paul Revere, Boston. Colored. Original. 9 x 10½ inches. Excessively rare and particularly so, colored. Slight time stains at upper-right and lower-left corners.

DESCRIPTION OF PRINT.

The view represents King Street with Faneuil Hall, and the Old South Church in back-ground; Butcher's Hall, with the Custom House to the right. British soldiers firing, three of their victims on the ground dead, with blood streaming from them, and two more being carried away wounded. A gun from Butcher's Hall is aiding in the slaughter.

Unhappy Boston! see thy Sons deplore,
Thy hallow'd Walks besmear'd with guiltless Gore.
While faithless P——n and his savage Bands,
With murdrous Rancour stretch their bloody Hands;
Like fierce barbarians grinning o'er their Prey,
Approve the Carnage and enjoy the Day.
If scalding drops from Rage from Anguish Wrung
Of speechless Sorrows lab'ring for a Tongue,
Or if a weeping World can ought appease
The plaintive Ghosts of Victims such as these:
The Patriot's copious Tears for each are shed,
A glorious Tribute which embalms the Dead
But know Fate summons to that awful Goal,
Where JUSTICE strips the murd'rer of his soul
Should venal C——ts the scandal of the Land
Snatch the relentless Villian from her Hand,
Keen Execrations on this Plate inscrib'd,
Shall reach a JUDGE who never can be brib'd.

The unhappy sufferers were Messrs. Sam'l Gray, Sam'l Maverick, Jam's Caldwell, Crispus Attucks and Pat'r Carr, Killed. Six wounded, two of them (Christ'r Monk and John Clark) mortally.

649 **Town and Harbor of Halifax, Nova Scotia.** Engraved by Mason, 1764. Folio. Line. 2 pieces.

650 **The Breach on the Walls of the Citadel at Palais.** Engraved by Canot Benoist, 1763. Folio. Line. 2 pieces.

651 **View of Roseau on the Island of Dominique,** with the attack made by Lord Rollo in 1760. Folio. Line.

652 **South-West View of Fort Royal, on the Island of** Guadaloupe. Engraved by Benazech, 1762. Folio. Line.

653 **St. Laurence. Six Elegant Views of the most** remarkable Places on the River and Gulf of St. Laurence. From the original, drawn on the spot by Capt. Hervey Smyth, Aid de Camp to Gen'l Wolfe. Engraved by Carot, Sandby, Elliot and others. Folio.
London, N. D. (1760.)
Brilliant impression. Very rare.

654 The Declaration of Independence of the United States of America. Painted by Jno. Trumbull. Engraved by A. B. Durand. Large folio. Line. Framed and glazed.

Original impression. Rare.

655 Perry's Victory on Lake Erie. Painted by T. Birch. Engraved by A. Lawson. Large folio. Line.

Proof before letters. Original impression. Very rare.

656 The Burning of the Theatre in Richmond, Virginia, on the night of the 26th Dec., 1811. Published Feb. 25, 1812, by B. Tanner, Philadelphia. 4to. Stipple. Colored. Rare.

657 New York, from Governor's Island. Engraved by Hill. Folio. Aquatint. Rare.

658 Battle of New Orleans. A Large and Spirited Aquatint, with Key of Explanation. Folio. Very rare.

659 Destruction of the Royal Statue at New York. Engraved by F. X. Habermann. Folio. Line. Colored. Rare.

660 Pennsylvania Hospital. Engraved by J. G. Exillious. Folio. Line.

661 Scull's Map of Philadelphia for 1750. Folio. Reprint.

662 Representation of the Figures Exhibited and Paraded through the streets of Philadelphia, on Saturday, the 30th of Sept., 1780. 4to. Reprint.

663 Nave di Amerigo Vespvcci Intermedio Quatro. Engraved by Giulio Parigi, 1608. 4to. Line. Very curious.

664 Manner on which the American Colonies Declared themselves Independent. Engraved by Nobles. Folio. Line.

665 Defeat and Death of Gen'l Braddock in North America. Engraved by Scott. Folio. Line.

666 New York, The South Prospect of the City of, in North America. From the *London Magazine*, 1761. Folio. Scarce.

667 Boston, a View of the City of. The Capital of New England, From the *London Magazine*. Folio. Rare.

668 Oswego, a South View of, on Lake Ontario. From the *London Magazine*, 1760. Folio.

669 Quebec, View of Cape Rouge above the City of. From Middleton's Geography. Folio. Line.

670 Three Allegorical Designs. Original. "Reconciliation of Great Britain and America." 3 pieces.

671 Declaration of Independence. Engraved by Illman & Pilbrow. 8vo. Line.

672 An Indian Cacique of the Island of Cuba addressing Columbus concerning a future state. Engraved by Bartolozzi. 4to. Stipple.

673 Capture of Andre. Engraved by W. E. Tucker. 12mo. Line.

674 Lafayette, Illustrations from the Life of. Lithographs. 6 pieces. 12mo. Rare.

675 President's House in Washington, destroyed by the British. From the *Lady's Magazine*, 1814. 8vo.

676 Culford, the Seat of the Marquis Cornwallis. 8vo. Line.

677 Battle of Bunker's Hill. Two Rare Old Prints. 12mo.

678 First Action between the English and Americans, at Concord, in 1775. 8vo, colored. Rare.

Rare American Maps.

679 Charleston. A Sketch of the Operations before Charleston, the capital of South Carolina, in 1780. A very elaborate map, large folio.

680 Massachusetts. A Sketch of the Harbor of Cape Cod. By Wm. Hogg, master in the Royal Navy. 1774 to 1776. Original drawing. Large folio.

681 New Jersey. Plan of the Operations of Gen'l Washington against the King's troops in New Jersey. By Wm Faden, 1777. Folio.

682 Quebec. Plan of the City and Environs, with its Siege by the Americans. By Wm. Faden, 1776. Large folio.

683 Lake Champlain. A Survey of. By Wm. Brassier. 1762. Large folio. Published in 1776.

684 Trinidad. Map of the Island of. Made by F. Mallet, 1802. Large folio, in 4 sheets.

685 New York. A Plan of the Operation of the King's Army under the command of Wm. Howe, in New York and East New Jersey. Engraved by Wm. Faden. 1777. Large folio.
Very important military map.

686 New York. A Map of the Province of New York, with part of Pennsylvania and New England. By Jno. Montresor. Very large folio.
The most important map of New York published in the eighteenth century.

687 New York. A Map of the Province of. By Claude Joseph Sauthier. Large folio.

687½ New Jersey. The Province of. By Wm Faden 1777. Large folio.
Small piece torn out of the top.

Miscellaneous Portraits.

688 Capt. Richard Farmer. Engraved by Murphy.
     Mezzotint. Folio. Brilliant proof.

689 John Bunyan. Engraved by Wm Sharp. 4to. Line.
     Brilliant impression.

690 Goethe. Engraved by Theo. Wright. Folio. Line.
     Proof.

691 Sir Thomas Morgan, Bart, Cromwell, Marlborough,
     Abercrombie, etc. 8 prints.

English Statesmen.

692 Lord George Germain. Engraved by Jacobe. Folio.
     Mezzotint. Fine and rare.

693 Frederick, Lord North. Engraved by T. Burke.
     Folio. Mezzotint. Fine and rare.

694 Sir Robert Liston. Engraved by Jno. Young. Folio.
     Full margin. Mezzotint. Brilliant proof.

695 Marquis of Lansdowne. Engraved by Bartolozzi. 4to.
     Full margin. Stipple. Proof. Rare.

696 Hon. Isaac Barre. Engraved by Jno. Hall. Folio.
     Full margin. Line. Fine and rare.

697 Catharine Macaulay. Engraved by J. Spilsbury.
     Folio. Mezzotint. Fine and rare.
     Author of several Tracts in favor of the American Revolution.

698 Israel Maudit, Lord North, Lord Shelburne, etc.
     6 portraits.

699 Charles Carroll of Carrollton. Lithograph by Childs and Inman. 4to.

700 50 Prints. Views in Philadelphia. Some rare.

701 50   "   "   "   "   "   "

702 50   "   "   "   "   "   "

703 50   "   "   "   "   "   "

704 34 American Portraits. Some rare.

705 3 Old English Caricatures.

706 Death of General Wolf. Engraved by Guttenberg. Folio. Line. Rare.

707 Upper Ferry Bridge, Philadelphia. By Geo Lehman. Colored aquatint. 4to.

708 88 Engravings for Illustrating "Baker's American Engravers."

Broadsides.

709 The Declaration of Independence. An Anastatic Copy on Parchment from the original. Framed and glazed.

This (we may say) is the present copy of the Declaration of Independence, as for all Historical purposes, most important even to the original, to be made thus, they utilized the original document to the most perfect extent; a certain process, which enabled the printer to get the facsimile impression of the press, for which no [illegible] from the original. That this [illegible] [illegible] people is the original Declaration, only [illegible] to those [illegible] [illegible] [illegible] [illegible] hardly description to the transference which [illegible] [illegible] [illegible] [illegible] [illegible] up with the [illegible], and from [illegible] they were [illegible] [illegible] [illegible] [illegible] impressions, on vellum. This [illegible] [illegible] [illegible] [illegible] [illegible] [illegible] [illegible] what the Document is; that the [illegible] [illegible] [illegible] [illegible] [illegible] inches by 2 feet 1½ inches, and is [illegible] [illegible] [illegible] [illegible] [illegible] [illegible] timbers of Independence Hall, [illegible] [illegible] [illegible] [illegible] [illegible] [illegible] stairway.

First Printed Copy of the Declaration of Independence.

710 **Broadside.** The first appearance in print of the Declaration of Independence. Being one of the few copies that were printed by Congress, and attested to by Charles Thomson, Secretary, before it was adopted for the purpose of sending it to each of the Thirteen States interested. Folio. Philadelphia: Printed by John Dunlap.

<small>Excessively rare, and we may also say unique, clean as the day of issue, and the rarest Broadside in existence relating to the American Revolution</small>

711 **Broadside.** The WAY to WEALTH, As clearly shewn in the *preface* of an old *Pennsylvanian (sic) Almanack*, intitled, *Poor Richard Improved*. Written by Dr. *Benjamin Franklin*. LONDON: *printed for* J. JOHNSON, No. 72, *St. Paul's Church-Yard* [1779:] *large folio, printed in 4 broad columns*.

The following curious editorial *Note* is printed within brackets at the bottom of the first column:

<small>"[Dr. Franklin, wishing to collect into one piece all the sayings upon the following subjects, which he had dropped in the course of publishing the Almanacks called *Poor Richard;* introduces *Father Abraham* for this purpose. Hence it is, that Poor Richard is so often quoted, and that, in the present title, he is said to be *Improved*.——Notwithstanding the stroke of humour in the concluding paragraph of this address, Poor Richard [Saunders] and Father Abraham have proved in America, that they are no *common* preachers. And, shall we, brother Englishmen, refuse good sense and saving knowledge, because it comes from the other side of the water?]"</small>

<small>This is a genuine copy of the original English Broadside reprint of these famous *Proverbs*, which is particularly described by Franklin in his *Autobiography*.</small>

712 **Broadside.** IN CONGRESS, May 14, 1777. Resolved, That the Quarter-Master General of the Army be authorized and empowered to appoint one Commissary of Forage for the Army, and one for each of the military departments thereof, with such and so many Forage-Masters as he shall judge necessary. * * * That Major-General Mifflin be allowed for his services as Quarter-Master General One Hundred and Sixty-six Dollars per month, in addition to his pay as Major-General. That the pay of a Deputy Quarter-Master General of a grand division of the Army be Seventy-five Dollars per month. That the pay of an Assistant Deputy Quarter-Master General be Forty Dollars per month, and that he have the rank of Captain. That the

pay of a Wagon-Master General be Seventy-five Dollars per month. That the pay of a Deputy Wagon-Master General be Fifty Dollars per month. That the pay of a Barrack-Master General be Seventy-five Dollars per month. That the pay of a Wagon-Master or Conductor of Wagons be Forty Dollars per month. That the pay of a Forage-Master be Forty Dollars per month, etc.

EXTRACT *from the* MINUTES.
CHARLES THOMSON, SECRETARY.

Folio. 2 pages. Full margin. Philadelphia. Printed by John Dunlap, 1777.

Rare.

713 Broadside. IN CONGRESS, June 10, 1777. Resolved, I. That for supplying the army of the United States with provisions, one Commissary-General and four Deputy Commissaries General of Purchases; and one Commissary General and three Deputy Commissaries General of Issues, be appointed by Congress. * * * XL. That the Commissary and Deputy Commissaries General of Purchases in each department, and every Purchaser employed under them, shall take the Oath of Fidelity to the United States, and the following oath or affirmation, viz.: " I ———— do solemnly and sincerely swear (or affirm) in the presence of Almighty God, that I will not collude with any person or persons whatever, to enhance the price of provisions or any article of commerce which I shall at any time hereafter be directed to purchase for the use of the United States, and that I will endeavor, by every honest means in my power, to procure the article which I may be directed to purchase at the most reasonable rates, and that I will not charge the public with any advance on any purchases by me made, and that I will in all things conduct myself as becometh a faithful servant of the public," etc.

EXTRACTS *from the* MINUTES. *Published by order of* CONGRESS.

CHARLES THOMSON, SECRETARY.

Folio. 4 pages. Full margin. Philadelphia. Printed by Jno. Dunlap. 1777.

Very rare.

714 **Broadside.** In Congress, September 26, 1778.
Resolved,
That a house be provided at the city or place where Congress shall sit, wherein shall be held the several offices of the Treasury.

That there be the following offices, viz.: The Comptroller's, Auditor's, Treasurer's, and two Chambers of Accounts; that each Chamber of Accounts consist of three Commissioners and two clerks, to be appointed by Congress.

That in the Treasurer's office there be a Treasurer annually appointed by Congress, and one clerk appointed by the Treasurer, etc.

(Followed by blank form to be used in the department.)

That in the blanks of the forms above written, no figures be used either for date or sum, but that the same be distinctly and plainly set in word at length, and without erasures or interlineations.

Extract from the minutes.
CHARLES THOMSON, *Secretary.*
[Philada., 1778.]

Folio, full margin.

715 **Broadside.** Oath of Allegiance. In Congress, February 3, 1778.
Resolved,
That every officer who holds or shall hereafter hold a commission or office from Congress, shall take and subscribe the following oath or affirmation:

"I, ———, do acknowledge the United States of America to be Free, Independent and Sovereign States, and declare that the people thereof own no allegiance or obedience to George the Third, King of Great Britain, and I renounce, refuse and abjure any allegiance or obedience to him; and I do swear (or affirm) that I will, to the utmost of my power, support, maintain, and defend the said United States against the said King George the Third, his heirs and successors, and his and their abbettors, assistants and adherents, and will serve the said United States in the office of ——— which I now hold, with fidelity, according to the best of my skill and understanding, so help me God."

That all officers of the army shall take and subscribe the foregoing oath of affirmation, before the Commander-in-Chief, or any Major-General, or Brigadier-General.

That all officers of the navy shall take and subscribe the same before one of the Commissioners of the Navy Boards, or before a Judge or Justice of the Peace of the State wherein they respectfully reside or shall receive their commissions or warrants, etc.

Extract from the minutes.

CHARLES THOMSON, Secretary.

[Philada., 1778.]

Folio, full margin.

716 **Broadside** In Congress, April 14, 1777.
Resolved.

That it be recommended to the Executive Power of each of the United States to enquire into the conduct of all officers on the recruiting service within them respectively; to remove all such as belong to the Battalions of their respective quota, who have neglected their duty or abused the trust reposed in them, and shall be found within their respective jurisdiction, and to fill up all vacancies which may happen by such removals; to transmit to Congress all such testimony as shall be taken against any Officer or Officers, who may have marched or removed from the State to whose Battalion he or they belong; and against any Officer or Officers belonging to the quota of another State who may have been guilty of neglect or misbehavior in the State where the enquiry shall be made.

That it be recommended to the said Executive Powers to procure exact returns of the Continental Troops in each State and transmit the same to Congress without delay, and all Officers and Soldiers of the Continental Army are hereby required to pay the strictest regard to the order of the Executive Powers of the several States touching the aforesaid premises, etc., etc.

Extract from the Minutes.

CHARLES (*sic.*) THOMSON, Secretary.

Philadelphia, Printed by John Dunlap. (1777.)

Folio. Full margin.

Rare.

717 **Broadside.** In Congress, July 30, 1779. Ordinance for establishing a Board of Treasury, and the proper Officers for managing the Finances of these United States. The Principal Officers of the Board shall consist of three Commissioners not members of Congress

and two members of Congress, and three of whom to form a board for the dispatch of business. The Commissioners shall be annually appointed by Congress and continue in Office until a new election. No member of Congress shall continue to serve as a member of the said board longer than six months by virtue of one appointment, nor shall there be more than one member of the said board at any time belonging to the same State. The board to have a Seal of Office, a Secretary, a Clerk and messenger. The Secretary to be annually appointed by Congress, the Clerk and Messenger by the board, etc., etc.

Extract from the Minutes.

CHARLES THOMSON, *Secretary*.

Folio. Full margin. (Phila.) 1779.

Very rare.

718 **Broadside.**—By the United States in Congress assembled, a proclamation Jan. 23, 1783. Elias Boudirot, President; declaring a Treaty of Amity and Commerce with Holland. 2 pages. Folio.

Rare.

719 **Broadside.**—In Congress, May 21, 1776. Resolutions relating to the Commissary General of Prisoners Department. Printed by John Dunlap, Phila., 1776. Folio, 3 pages.

The copy that formerly belonged to Elias Boudint, Commissary General of Prisoners, with inscription on the back and correction in the body in his handwriting

720 **Certificate** of Enlistment as a Waggoner or Team Driver in the Army of the United States, 1778. "This is to certify, that * * * hath enlisted himself as a waggoner or team-driver in the Army of the United States, to serve for * * * unless sooner discharged, in consideration whereof he is to receive pay at the rate of Ten Pounds per month, and one ration per day, and in case the said * * * shall produce a certificate from the Waggon-master General of his good behavior after six months' service, he shall receive a suit of clothes by Way of Bounty, provided his Enlistment be for one year or upwards. In Witness whereof the said * * * and * * * who is empowered to enlist Waggoners, have hereunto interchangeably set their Hands * * * Day of * * * 1778." Small 4to.

Very rare.

721 **Broadsides.** Administration of Robert Morris. A General View of Receipts and Expenditures of Public Monies, by authority from the Superintendent of Finance, from the time of his entering on the Administration of the Financers, to the 31st December, 1781, and from 1st of January, 1782 to the 1st of January 1783. Folio, full margin. 2 pieces N. P. A. D.

Very rare.

722 **Grant, Gen'l U. S.** Autograph Letter, Signed. City Point, Va., July 17, 1864. 8vo, 2 pages.

"Messrs. Rockhill & Wilson
  Dear Sirs
    Your letter of the 12th inst including one from L. J. Livermore, Chairman of one of the Committees of the Philad. Sanitary Fair, asking directions for the shipment of a suit of clothes which your partiality and that of many loyal citizens of Philadelphia have donated for the benefit of myself; the subscriptions giving to the benefit of the sick and wounded Soldiers, is received.
    Please forward them to me through Adams Express.
      I am
        Very respectfully
         Your obt Svt
         U. S. Grant
         Lt Gen U. S. A."

723 **Grant's** Order for His First Suit of Civilian Clothing After the War. Autograph Letter, Signed by Gen'l U. S. Grant. Headquarters Armies of the United States, Niagara Falls, N. Y., Aug. 9, 1865. 4to.

"Messrs. Rockhill & Wilson
  Dear Sirs
    Please make and forward to me at Galena Ill. a suit of Citizen clothing, charges to be collected on delivery. I want a Dark Brown frock coat, the pants and vest of some light cloth of such color as you may select.
    I will be in Galena in about one week from to day and would like to receive this clothing as soon as possible.
        Yours truly
         U. S. Grant
         Lt. Gen'"

724 **Brown, Jno.** Celebrated Abolitionist, Executed at Harper's Ferry. Autograph Letter, Signed. Akron, Ohio, March 20, 1852. 4to.

Rare.

725 **The Same.** Autograph Letter, Signed. Elisabethtown N. Y., Feb 6, 1852. 4to.

Rare American History.

726 **Society** of the Cincinnati. Observations on a late pamphlet entitled "Considerations upon the Society or Order of the Cincinnati," clearly evincing the innocence and propriety of that honorable and respectable institution, in answer to vague conjectures, false insinuations and ill-founded objections. By an obscure individual [Ædanus Burke]. 8vo. Robt. Bell, Philadelphia, 1783.

The rarest Tract on the Society of the Cincinnati; contains "The Plan for establishing the Society or Order of the Cincinnati."

727 **Court-Martial** of Gen'l Schuyler. Proceedings of a General Court-Martial. Held at Major-General Lincoln's Quarters, near Quaker Hill, in the State of New York, by order of his *Excellency, General Washington,* Commander-in-Chief of the Army of the United States of America, for the trial of Major-General Schuyler, Oct. 1, 1778, Major-General Lincoln, president. Folio. Original covers. Hall & Sellers, Philadelphia, 1778.

Fine copy of this exceedingly scarce trial.

728 **Constitution** of the United States. 8vo sheep.
Boston, 1785

729 **Lee, Gen. Chas.** the Life of. 8vo boards, uncut.
New York, 1813.

730 **Shakespeare, Wm.** Plays and Poems of. First American Edition. 8 vols. Original contemporary, calf. Gilt canary edges.
Bioren and Madan, Philadelphia 1796.

A fine copy of this excessively rare work.

731 **Evans Lewis.** A Geographical, Historical, etc. Essays, Analysis of a General Map of the Middle British Colonies. 4th Original one-half binding.
Franklin & Hall, Philadelphia, 1755.

With the excessively rare original map, also another scarce early map inserted.

732 **Las Casas,** Bartholomew. The Spanish Colonie, or brief Chronicle of the Acts and Gestes of the Spaniards in the West Indies, called the New World, for the space of XL yeeres written in the Castilean Tongue, and nowe first translated into English by M. M. S. Small 4th Full dark blue crushed levant tooled to a Roger Payne pattern, by W. Pratt.
Imprinted at London for W. Brome, 1583.

Fine copy. The excessively rare first English Edition of Las Casas. We cannot trace the sale of any copy.

733 **Symonds William.** Virginia, a Sermon preached 25th April, 1609. Small 4to. Full crushed red levant, super extra gilt by F. Bedford.
London. Printed by I. Windet, 1609.

One of the very earliest tracts relating to Virginia in existence.

734 **St. Clair, Arthur.** Narrative of the manner in which the campaign against the Indians in 1791 was conducted. 8vo. Boards. Uncut. Philadelphia, 1812.

735 **Heath, William.** Memoirs of Major-General Heath. 8vo. Sheep. Boston, 1798

The rare original edition.

736 **Burgoyne, General.** State of the expedition from Canada. Second edition, with maps. 8vo. Half morocco gilt. London, 1780

Fine copy. Rare.

737 **Virginia.** A Declaration of the State and the Affairs of the Colony in Virginia, with the names of the Adventurers. Small 4to. Full crushed levant, super extra gilt by F. Bedford. London, 1620

Very choice copy of this exceedingly scarce work.

738 **Cruxius, Francois.** Historiae Canadensis. 4to. Full green crushed levant by Champole-Duru.
Paris, 1664

All the plates in perfect condition, including also the folding plate of the Martyrdom of the Jesuits, which is almost always wanting.

739 **Wood, William.** New England's Prospect, with map. Small. Full Russia. Neat. London, 1635

The corner-stone of New England History. One of the rarest pieces of Americana. The map and book in fine condition.

740 **Mather, Increase.** A brief history of the war with the Indians in New England. Small 4to. Full crushed blue levant, super extra gilt by F. Bedford. London, 1676

From the Menzie Sale.

741 **Las Casas.** Bartholomew. Narratio Regionum Indicarum. With all the plates. Small 4to. Full crushed blue levant, by W. Pratt. Francfort, 1698.

Fine copy of the Latin edition of this very curious tract.

742 **Botta, Chas.** History of the War of the Independence of the United States. 3 vols., 8vo, sheep. Philadelphia, 1821.

743 **Winterbotham, Wm.** Historical View of the United States, with Portraits of Washington, Franklin, Penn, and the Author. 4 vols., 8vo, sheep. London, 1795.

744 **Pickering, Jno.** Vocabulary of Words and Phrases peculiar to the United States. 8vo, boards, uncut. Boston, 1816.

745 **Monardes, Nicolas.** Joyfull Newes of the Newefound Worlde. Illustrated with wood-cuts. Small 4to. Full Polished red levant, morocco. Extra Gilt, by F. Bedford. London, 1596.

Fine copy of this excessively scarce work.

746 **Virginia.** The New Life of Virginia. Small 4to. Full crushed red levant morocco super extra gilt by F. Bedford. London, 1612.

Very choice copy of one of the rarest tracts on Virginia.

747 **New Jersey.** A Bill in Chancery, at the Suite of John, Earl of Stair, and other Proprietors of Eastern Division of New Jersey, against Benj. Bond, and some other Clinker Lot Right Men, with three large maps. Folio. Full crushed olive levant, super extra gilt, by W. Pratt. Jas. Parker, New York, 1747.

Contains all the maps—a very fine copy.

748 **Pennsylvania.** Penn vs. Baltimore. In Chancery. Breviate. John Penn, Thos. Penn, and Richard Penn, Esquire, *Plaintiffs*; Chas. Calvert, Esquire, Lord Baltimore, *Defendant*. Folio three-quarter crushed red levant, gilt backs burnished gilt edges, by W. Pratt.
London (about 1740).

> The rarity of this volume is only exceeded by its importance as a contribution to the History of Pennsylvania. It contains a full history of the dispute about the boundary between Pennsylvania and Maryland, and having been printed only for the use of the English Court of Chancery, is one of the rarest books relating to America.

749 **Anburey, Thos.** Travels through the Interior Parts of America. 2 volumes, 8vo. Three-quarter Sprinkled Calf Gilt, canary edges. London 1791.

Fine copies with all the plates.

750 **Ward, Ned.** A trip to Jamaica, with a true character of the People and Island. Folio. London 1700.

An excessively rare and scurrilous pamphlet, in which he portrays in very free language, the character of the female inhabitants.

751 **Free-Masons.** The Constitution of the, containing the History, Charges, Regulations, etc., of that most Ancient and Right Worshipful Fraternity. For the use of the Lodges. Small 4to. Original Calf. Broken.
B. Franklin, Phila., 1734.

752 **Monthly Miscellany, The.** The Earliest New Jersey Magazine, from Jan. to Dec. 1759, wanting October. 11 Parts. 8vo. uncut. Woodbridge, N. J., 1759.

Excessively rare, and almost unique in this condition, abounding with interesting items of Colonial and Indian History. Printed by Jas. Parker.

753 **Wholesome Water in Philadelphia.** Report of the Committee for the introduction of. 8vo.
Philada., 1801.

754 **Reid, Arthur.** Reminiscences of the Revolution, or Le Loup's Bloody Trail from Salem to Fort Edward. 8vo.
Utica, 1859.

755 **Latrobe, Jno. H. B.** History of Mason and Dixon's Line. 8vo. Philada., 1855.

756 Robinson, Fayette. California and its Gold Regions, with a Geographical and Topographical View of the Country. 8vo. uncut. New York, 1849.

757 Peter Pindar. The Trial of Doctor John Wolcot, otherwise Peter Pindar, Esq., for Criminal Conversation with the wife of Mr. Knight of the Royal Navy, before Rgt. Hon. Lord Ellenborough, June 27, 1807, with the Rare Folding Plate and the Hieroglyphical Letter. 8vo, uncut. London, (1807).

Rare.

758 Constitution and Ordinances of the City of Philadelphia. 8vo. Philada., 1790.

759 Unique Copy of the Journals of the House of Representatives of the Commonwealth of Pennsylvania, Beginning the twenty-Eighth Day of November 1776, and Ending the Second Day of October, 1781, with the Proceedings of the Several Committees and Conventions before and at the Commencement of the American Revolution. Vol. 1. Folio. Original boards. Totally uncut. Philadelphia: Printed by John Dunlap, 1782.

This volume (unique in this shape) is exceedingly scarce in any condition. The few copies known are all cut down to very narrow borders. Therefore, we do not hesitate in declaring it to be unique. It is uncut in every particular—having a margin all round of two inches, and as clean as the day of issue. The assertion that it is the most important work published relating to the transactions of the Revolutionary Government, 1774-1781, the following extract from the first page will substantiate:

"State of Pennsylvania, | In General Assembly, | Monday, April 2, 1781 | *Resolved* | That Michael Hilligas, Esquire, be requested and empowered to revise, com | —pare, correct and publish in one Volume. The Resolves of the Committee of the | late Province of Pennsylvania, with their Instructions to their Representatives in Assem— | bly, held at Philadelphia, The Fifteenth Day of July, One Thousand Seven Hundred | and Seventy-four; The Proceedings of the Convention for the Province of Pennsylva— | nia, held at Philadelphia, the Twenty-third day of January, one Thousand Seven | Hundred and Seventy-five; the Proceedings of the Provincial Conference of Commit | tees, held at Carpenter's Hall, in the City of Philadelphia, The Eighteenth Day of | June, One Thousand Seven Hundred and Seventy-Six; The Declaration of Indepen— | dence by the Congress of the United States, made the Fourth Day of July, One Thou— | sand Seven Hundred and Seventy-six; The Minute of the Proceedings of the Conven | tion of the State of Pennsylvania, held at Philadelphia, the Fifteenth day of July, One | Thousand Seven Hundred and Seventy-six, with the Constitution; The Minutes of the | Assemblies of the Commonwealth of Pennsylvania to the end of the present year, and | the Articles of Confederation of the United States of America, and | That the House will purchase and pay for Two Hundred Copies thereof, | *Extract from the Minutes*, | SAMUEL STERETT, *Clerk*."

Most of the original papers from which this book was composed have been destroyed, so this is the only official data that we have of those valuable documents, and is the first time that it has ever been offered at public sale. It was formerly the property of Benj. Spyker, one of the Committee of the

Provincial Conference of the Province of Pennsylvania, held at Carpenter's Hall, Philadelphia, June 18, 1776, and has his name inscribed on the back cover in pen and ink, in large old English style letters.

It is also important, as it contains copies of all the Broadsides issued by the Provisional Congress.

760 **Constitution**, The, proposed for the Government of the United States of America, by the Federal Convention, held at Philadelphia, in the year one thousand seven hundred and eighty-seven, to which is annexed the ratification thereof by the Delegates of Pennsylvania in the State Convention. 8vo, original covers, uncut. Philadelphia: printed by Hall & Sellers, 1787.

The first appearance of the Constitution in pamphlet form, and of the greatest rarity. Fine clean copy.

761 **Constitution** of the Commonwealth of Pennsylvania as altered and amended by the Convention for that purpose, freely chosen and assembled and by them proposed for the consideration of their constituents. 8vo, original cover, uncut. Philadelphia, printed by Zachariah Poulson, Jr., 1790.

Very rare. The only copy of the few that are known that contains on the page facing the title an extract from the minutes of the Convention. On the question—"Shall the Constitution as agreed to in Convention, be published for the consideration of the good people of Pennsylvania?" The names of the members being called over, it appeared that the question was unanimously determined in the affirmative, Friday, February 26, 1790."
The first appearance in pamphlet form of the Constitution of Pennsylvania.

762 **The Same.** In German. 8vo, uncut.
Philadelphia, Gedrucktbey Melchior Steiner, 1790.

Equally as rare as the English edition.

763 **Early Imprint.** The Inflexible Captive. A Tragedy by Miss Hannah Moore. The third edition. 12mo. Bristol printed. Philadelphia: reprinted for John Sparhawk, by James Humphreys, Jr., 1774.

Unknown to Bibliographs of Early Philadelphia printed Plays.

764 **Penn and Mead Trial.** The People's Antient and just Liberties asserted in the Tryal of Wm. Penn and Wm. Mead, at the Sessions held at the Old Baily in London, the first, third, fourth, and fifth of Sep., 1670, against the most arbitrary procedure of that Court. Small 4to, half-morocco, uncut. London, 1670.

765 Smyth, J. F. D. A Tour in the United States of America, containing an account of the present situation of that country. The Population, Agriculture, Commerce, Customs, and Manners of the Inhabitants. Anecdotes of several members of the Congress and General Officers in the American Army. 2 vols. 8vo, calf (cracked). London, 1784.

Contains a very searching review of the character of General Washington, pp. 143-150, Vol. II. Each volume has the autograph of "W. Hamilton, 1785" on the title.

766 Burning of the Richmond Theatre. Narrative and Report of the Causes and Circumstances of the Deplorable Conflagration at Richmond, (Virginia). From Letters and Authentic Documents. 16mo, original boards. Printed for the public, Jan. 12, 1812.

767 Dickinson, Jonathan. Narrative of a Shipwreck in the Gulph of Florida in 1699. 16mo, boards.
Burlington, 1811.

768 Deane, Silas. An Address to the United States of North America, to which is added a letter to the Hon. Robt. Morris. 8vo, uncut. London, 1784.

769 Address and Recommendations to the State by the United States in Congress Assembled. 8vo, uncut. Philadelphia. Printed by David C. Claypoole, 1783.

This scarce pamphlet contains valuable information relative to the Revolutionary Army, transmitted through Gen. Geo. Washington.

770 Dissertation on the Political Union and Constitution of the Thirteen United States of North America, which is necessary to their Preservation and Happiness, humbly offered to the Public by a citizen of Philadelphia. 8vo, uncut. Philadelphia: Printed and sold by T. Bradford, 1783.

771 Journals of Congress from Wednesday, March 31st, to Saturday, April 10th; Monday, April 12th to Saturday, April 17; Saturday, April 24th, to Monday, May 3d; Saturday, May 1st, to Monday, May 10th; Monday, May 10th, to Saturday, May 15th, 1779.
Five pamphlets, 8vo, uncut, as issued.
Philada. Printed by David C. Claypoole, 1779.

772. **Three** Letters addressed to Public, on the following subjects: I. The Nature of the Federal Union.—The Powers vested in Congress, and therein of Sovereignty. II. The Civil and Military Powers.—The Dispute between General Greene and Governor Gerard, respecting Flags of Truce. III. The Public Debt.—The Act of Confederation defective; a remedy suggested.—The Five per cent. Impost Act considered and recommended? 8vo, uncut. Philada. Printed by T. Bradford, 1783.

Signed "Tullius," and dated Charles Town, May 5, 1783.

773. **(Raynal, Abbe.)** The Sentiments of a Foreigner on the Disputes of Great Britain and America. Translated from the French. 8vo, uncut. Original covers. Philada. Printed by James Humphrey, 1775.

774. **War** in America, An Impartial History of the, between Great Britain and the United States. With portrait of John Hancock, by Norman. Vol. 1. Part 1. Original covers, uncut. Boston, 1781.

775. **Caldwell, Chas.** An Oration commemorative of the Character and Administration of Washington, delivered Feb'y 22, 1810. 8vo, uncut. Philada., 1810.

776. **Breck, Sam'l.** Sketch of the Internal Improvements already made in Pennsylvania. Illustrated with maps. 8vo, original covers, uncut. Philada., 1818.

777. **View** of Fairmount. Report of the Watering Committee to the Select and Common Councils of the City of Philadelphia, Jan. 9, 1823, with folding plate of Fairmount Water Works, and other illustrations. 8vo, original cover. Philada., 1823.

778. **Long, Major Stephen** H. Account of An Expedition from Pittsburgh to the Rocky Mountains, performed in the years 1819 and '20. Compiled by Edwin James. 2 vols., 8vo, original bds., uncut. Philada., 1823.

Text only. Name of former owner on title. Somewhat foxed.

779. **Weems, M. L.** The Life of Benj. Franklin, with many choice anecdotes. Illustrated. 12mo, sheep. Philada., 1835.

780 Ruxton, George F. Adventures in Mexico and the Rocky Mountains. 2 vols. 12mo. Original covers, uncut. New York, 1848

781 Collection of State Papers Relative to the First Acknowledgment of the Sovereignty of the United States of America, and the Reception of their Minister Plenipotentiary, by their High Mightinesses the States General of the United Netherlands, to which is prefixed the political character of John Adams, by an American, likewise an essay on Canon and Federal Law, by John Adams. 8vo, paper, uncut.
London, 1782

782 Journal of the First Session of the Tenth House of Representatives of the Commonwealth of Pennsylvania, which commenced at Lancaster on Tuesday, the third day of December, in the year of our Lord, 1799. Folio, uncut.
Lancaster, printed by Francis and Robt. Bailey, 1799

A portion of the lower margin of the title and first two pages missing.
Contains also Receipts and Expenditures in the Treasury of Pennsylvania from Jan. to Dec., 1799, and report of the Register-General of the State of the finances of Pennsylvania for 1799. Wanting the last two pages.

783 Journal of the Senate of the Commonwealth of Pennsylvania, which commenced at Lancaster, on Tuesday, the third day of December, in the year 1799. Folio. Original cover, uncut.
Printed by William Hamilton, Lancaster, 1800.

Contains also Report of the Register General of the State of the Finances of Pennsylvania, for 1799, and Receipts and Expenditures in the Treasury of the Commonwealth of Pennsylvania for 1799.

784 Morris, Robt. A statement of the accounts of the United States of America, during the Administration of the Superintendent of Finance, commencing with his appointment, on the 20th day of February, 1781, and ending with his resignation, on the first day of November, 1784. Folio. Original old calf binding.
Philadelphia, printed by Robert Aitken, at the Pope's Head, 1785.

Contains the address of Robt. Morris to the inhabitants of the United States. Reviewing the Finances of the country from February, 1781, to November, 1784. Also shows the cost of maintaining the American Army during the later portion of the Revolutionary war.
Very rare. Magnificent copy. Clean as the day of issue

785 **Jones, William A.** Memorial of the late Honorable David S. Jones, with an appendix, containing notices of the Jones family, of Queen's County, N. Y. Small 4to, cloth. New York: 1849. *Very rare, a small edition only printed.*

> Mr. Jones is also the author of a delightful series of Essays on old English poets, published under the title of "Characters and Criticisms," N. Y., 1857. 2 vols. 12mo.
> "Our most analytic, if not altogether our best critic, is Mr. William A. Jones."   EDGAR A. POE.

786 **Miller Laws of Pennsylvania.** The Charters and Acts of Assembly of the Province of Pennsylvania. Vol. I. Containing the Charters of the said Province, and the City, Boroughs and Towns thereof, the Titles of all the Laws of the said Province, since its first establishment down to the year 1700. The Acts of the said Assembly from the year 1700 to 1743, now in force, and the Royal Confirmations and Repeals of the said Act. Vol. II. Containing the Acts of Assembly of the said Province, from the year 1744 to 1759, now in force; a collection of all the Laws that have been formerly in force within this Province, for Regulating of Descents and Transferring the Property of Lands, but are since expired, altered, or repealed, from the establishment of the Province down to the present time, together with an index, referring to the matters contained in both the volumes. 2 vols. in 1, folio. Old calf.
Philadelphia: Printed by Peter Miller and Comp., 1762.

> Rare. Has autograph of John Morris, Jr., on title page. About a dozen pages water-stained. The "errata" which is often wanting, is here pasted on the inside of front cover.

787 **[Cobbett, Wm.]** A Bone to Gnaw for the Democrats; or Observations on a Pamphlet entitled "The Political Progress of Britain." By Peter Porcupine. Both parts complete. 2 pamphlets. 8vo, uncut.
Phila., 1795.

> Part 1 has the autograph of Benj. Morris on the Title and Part 2 that of Thos. Dundas.

788 **[Cobbett, Wm.]** A Little Plain English addressed to the People of the United States on the Treaty negotiated with his Britannic Majesty, and on the conduct of the President relative thereto in answer to "The Letter of Franklin," with a supplement containing an account of the turbulent and factious proceedings of the opposers of the Treaty. By Peter Porcupine. 8vo, uncut.
Phila., 1795.

789 [Cobbett, Wm.] A Kick for a Bite; or, Review upon Review: with a Critical Essay on the works of Mrs. S. Rowson. 8vo, uncut. Phila., 1795.

Has Autograph on Title of "Benj. Morris, March 1795."

790 [Cobbett, Wm.] The Democratiad: a Poem, in Retaliation for the "Philadelphia Jockey Club." By a gentleman of Connecticut. 8vo, uncut. Phila., 1795.

Very rare

" O Washington! how stands thy dauntless breast!
Do scenes like these disturb thy nightly rest?
Tho' Charleston mob, like lice in Egypt, swarms,
Tho' Rutledge rages, and tho' Pinkney storms;
Tho' Bache and Mason join to print, and sell
Tho' Hydrop Blair ' the treaty kick to hell."

Illustrious man! thy indignation shew,
And plunge them headlong where they ought to go."

791 Waldo S. Putnam. The Life and Character of Stephen Decatur, late Commodore and Post-Captain in the Navy of the United States. Second edition. Containing sketches of some distinguished contemporaries of Com. Decatur, a Naval Register, etc., with grouping of portraits of Bainbridge, Laurence, Decatur, Porter and Macdonough, and views of Naval Battles. 8vo. Sheep.
Middletown, Conn., 1821.

792 Weems, M. L. The Life of George Washington, with curious anecdotes, equally honorable to himself and exemplary to his young countrymen * * * Tenth edition. Greatly improved, embellished with seven engravings and a map of the United States. 12mo. Sheep.
Philadelphia: Printed for Matthew Carey. 1810.

Exceedingly scarce, as it is the only copy known that contains the map. The portrait of Washington is indicated in Baker, No. 328.

793 Mather, Cotton. The Wonders of the Invisible World | being an account of the | Tryals | of | Several Witches | lately Executed | in | New England | and of several remarkable curiosities therein occurring | together with | I. Observations upon the Nature, the Number and the Operations of the Devil | II. A short narrative of a late outrage committed by a knot of witches in | *Swede Land*, very much resembling, and so far explaining, that under which | *New England* has labored--III.

Some Councels directing a due improvement of the Terrible things lately | done by the unusual and amazing Range of *Evil-Spirits in New England* | IV. A brief discourse upon those *Temptations*, which are the more ordinary Devi | ces of Satan | 4to. Full light calf. Canary edges. By Pratt.

Printed first at Boston in New England, and reprinted at London, for John Dunton, at the Raven in the Poultry, 1693.

Last leaf repaired on the margin. Otherwise a fine copy. Very rare.

794 **Ward, Nathaniel.** The | Simple Cobler | of | Aggavvam in America | willing | To help 'mend his Native Country, la | mentably tattered, both in the upper-leather | and sole, with all the honest stitches he can take | And as willing never to bee paid for his work--by old English wonted pay | It is his trade to patch all the year long, gratis | Therefore, I pray Gentlemen keep your purses | By Theodore de la Guard. Small 4to, calf. London. Printed by Jno. Dever and Robert Ibbetson, for Stephen Rowtell, at the signe of the bible in Popes Head-Alley, 1647.

Very good copy. Exceedingly scarce.

795 **Andreana.** Vindication of the Captors of Major Andre. 16mo. Extended by insertions to Post 8vo. Full crimson crushed levant, gilt back, gold borders on side ; inside lined with crimson crushed levant sumptuously gilt and hand tooled by Matthews. Edges uncut, top edge gilt. New York, 1817.

Extra illustrated, with autograph letter, signed, of Judge E. Benson, and 18 rare engravings, including a very rare German Print of the Capture of Major André. Fine portrait of André by D. Berger. The exceedingly scarce portrait of Washington by A. W. Kuffner, 1793. A very rare portrait of La Fayette by C. Kobell. Scarce. Portraits of Baron De Steuben and Benedict Arnold and Chas. Thomson, by B Reading, 1783. Portrait of Gen'l Knox, with autograph inlaid under it. The scarce portrait of Sir Henry Clinton, engraved by F. Bartolozzi, 1780. Sir Henry Clinton's autograph inlaid on separate leaf. Portrait of Major Gen'l Greene, engraved by Jas. Neagle, and other rare prints.

796 **Washington, General.** Epistles, Domestic, Confidential and Official from ; written about the commencement of the American Contest, when he entered on the Command of the Army of the United States. With an interesting series of his Letters, particularly to the British Admirals, Arbuthnot and Digby, to Gen. Sir Henry Clinton, Lord Cornwallis, Sir Guy Carleton, Marquis de La Fayette, etc., etc., to Benjamin Har-

rison, Esq., Speaker of the House of Delegates in Virginia, to Admiral the Count de Grasse, General Sullivan, respecting an attack on New York; including many applications and addresses presented to him, with his answers; Orders and Instructions, on important occasions, to his Aids-de-Camp, etc., etc. None of which have been printed in the two volumes published a few months ago; with Portrait. 8vo. Contemporary Binding, New York. Printed by G. Robinson, corner of William and John Streets, and J. Bull, No. 115 Cherry Street, and sold by James Rivington, No. 156 Pearl Street. 1796.

Exceedingly Scarce. Contains the Very Rare Portrait by S. Hill. Full Bust in Uniform. Head three-quarters to the right, the order of the Cincinnati on the left breast. Oval, in a rectangle, with the inscription underneath, "George Washington, President of the United States of America." Engraved by S. Hill.
This Portrait agrees with Baker, No. 129, although he takes his description from the "Official Letters," 2d Edition, printed in Boston, 1796, and describes it as rare.

797 **First American Edition of Sterne.** The works of Laurence Sterne, A. M., Prebendary of York, and Vicar of Sutton in the Forest, and of Stellington, near York. With the Life of the Author. With the rare portrait. 5 vols., 12mo. Old calf.
Jas. Humphreys, Philadelphia, 1774.

This copy came from the Library of Robert Morris, and has the autographs of "Nancy Morris," "Samuel C. Morris, 1774." The latter appearing thoroughout the volumes no less than five times. The last volume has had the autograph cut from the title page, but without injury to the print Very rare.

798 **Aitken's General American Register**, and the Gentleman's and Tradesman's Complete Annual Account Book and Calendar, for the Year 1773. 12 mo, sheep. Tuck. J. Cruikshank, Philadelphia, 1773.

799 **Cobbett, Wm.** The Rush Light, by Peter Porcupine. Nos. 1 & 2, for Feby. 15 & 28, 1800. 8vo, uncut.
New York.

Contains scurrilous attacks on Dr. Rush, and other eminent personages. Very rare. With original covers.

800 **St. George.** Rules and Constitution of the Society of the Sons of St. George. 8vo. Original covers.
E. Oswald, Philadelphia, A. D., 1788.

Scarce. With list of members

801 **The Same.** 8vo. Philadelphia, 1797.

802 **The Same.** 8vo. Philadelphia, 1802.

803 **The Same.** 8vo. Corrected to 1814. Philadelphia, 1802.

804 **Trollope, Nicodemus.** The Scribes of Gotham. A Poem. 8vo. New York, 1833.

805 **Ford, Gov. Thomas.** A history of Illinois, from its commencement as a State in 1818 to 1847. Containing a full account of the Black Hawk war, the Rise, Progress and Fall of Mormonism, the Alton and Lovejoy Riots, and other important and interesting events. 8vo.
Chicago, 1854.

Scarce.

806 **Lewis, Meriwether.** The Travels of Capts. Lewis and Clarke, by order of the Government of the United States, performed in the years 1804, 1805 and 1806, being upwards of three thousand miles, from St. Louis, by way of the Missouri and Columbia Rivers, to the Pacifick Ocean, containing an account of the Indian Tribes who inhabit the western part of the continent unexplored and unknown before, with copious delineation of the manners, customs, religions, etc. of the Indians, to which is subjoined a summary of the statistical view of the Indian nations, from the official communication of, *embellished with a map of the country inhabited by the western tribes of Indians, and fine engravings of Indian chiefs.* 8vo sheep.
Philadelphia: Published by Hubbard Lester, 1809.

Fine copy. Exceedingly scarce. Has name of former owner on title page.

807 **Henry, John Joseph.** An account and interesting account of the hardships and sufferings of that band of heroes who traversed the wilderness in the campaign against Quebec in 1775. 12mo sheep. Lancaster; 1812

Rare.

808 **Boston Imprint.** The Safety of Appearing at the Day of Judgment in the Righteousness of Christ. Opened and applied by Solomon Stoddard. 8vo. Old calf. Boston: Reprinted for D. Hinchman at his shop at Corn Hill, 1729.

Somewhat water stained.

809 **Horry, Brig.-Gen'l P.** The life of General Francis Marion, a celebrated Partizan officer in the Revolutionary War against the British and Tories in South Carolina and Georgia. Second edition. 12mo. Sheep.
Baltimore, 1814

810 **Barlow, Joel.** Psalms carefully suited to the Christian worship in the United States of America, being an improvement of the old version of the Psalms of David, allowed by the Reverend Synod of New York and Philadelphia, to be used in churches and private families. 16mo, old calf. New York: Printed for Berry & Rogers and John Reid, 1792.

Scarce.

811 **Confederate Almanac.** The Confederate States Almanac for the year of our Lord 1862. Edited by T. O. Summers, D. D. 12mo, paper. Nashville, 1862

Contains five pages of "Memorabilia," giving the dates of battles and important events relating to the Confederacy, from Dec. 20, 1860, to Nov. 26, 1861.

812 **Methodist Conferences, Minutes of the.** Annually held in America from 1773 to 1813 inclusive. 12mo, sheep.
New York, 1813.

813 **Early Philadelphia Bible.** The Holy Bible, containing the Old and New Testaments translated out of the original Greek, 12mo, sheep.
Philadelphia. Printed by Wm. Young, 1794.

Wants title to the New Testament.

814 **Collection** of 216 War Envelopes. Good lot, including many rare varieties.

815 **Pennsylvania** Packet and Daily Advertiser, from Jan. 1 to Dec. 31, 1788. Folio. Philadelphia.
   This volume is particularly interesting for the rare reports on the ratification of the constitution.

816 **Carey's** Atlas to Guthrie's Geography. Wanting several maps, containing many rare American maps. Folio. Boards.

817 **Barlow**, Joel; Illustrations to the Columbiad. After paintings by R. Fulton, and Smirke. Eleven Plates and Portraits of Barlow. 4to, half roan.
   Contains Cornwallis surrendering his sword to Washington, Hester appearing to Columbus in prison, etc.

818 **Early** New York Opera. The Archers or Mountaineers of Switzerland. An opera in three acts, (composed by W. Dunlap,) as performed by the Old American Company in New York. New York, 1796
   First edition. Rare.

819 **Morris**, Capt. Thomas. Quashy, or, the Coal-Black Maid. A tale. 12mo. Philadelphia, 1797
   By Capt. Morris, of "The Plenipotentiary" fame.

820 **Mynehieur** von Herrick Heinelman. The Dancing-Master, or the Confluence of Nassau Street and Maiden Lane, as it was whilom, to which is added The Big Red Nose, and How to Bleech It. 12mo. New York, 1824

821 **Lee**, Charles. Memoirs of the Life of the late Second in Command in the Service of the United States of America during the Revolution. To which is added his Political and Military Essays. 8vo. Sheep.
   New York, 1793
   First edition. Rare.

822 **Franklin**, Imprint. A collection of the works of Thomas Chalkley. 2 vols. 8vo.
   Franklin & Hall, Philadelphia, 1749

823 **Transactions** of the American Philosophical Society. Held at Philadelphia for promoting useful knowledge. Vol. 1. January, 1769, to January, 1771. 4to, half bound.
   W. & T. Bradford, Philadelphia, 1771
   Exceedingly scarce. Contains a rare map of New Jersey.

Addenda

To Sale December 15 and 16, 1891.

510 **Broadside.** Proclamation dated Nov. 20, 1782. Signed by John Dickinson. Folio.

<small>Relative to the observance of Sunday.</small>

511 **Broadside.** Letter of Marque. Issued by Congress in 1777. Folio.

512 **Broadside.** The inconveniences that have happened to some persons which have transported themselves from England to *Virginia*, without provisions necessary to sustain themselves, hath greatly hindered the Progress of that noble Plantation, for the prevention of the like disorders * * * * It is thought requisite to publish this short declaration * * * * etc. Folio. Full margin. Very rare. London, 1622.

513 **Broadside.** Receipts for Provisions, etc., for the supply of Her Majesty's forces within the Province of Massachusetts Bay in New England. Dated May 29, 1710. Signed by Andrew Belcher, Commissary-General. Folio.

514 **Broadside.** A Bill to Enable His Majesty to Grant Commissions to a certain number of foreign Protestants * * * to act and rank as Officers and Engineers in America, only * * * 3 pages. Folio. No date (Temp. George II.)

515 **Broadside.** Grand Celebration of the Abolition of the Slave Trade. Caricature. Folio. No date.

516 **Broadside.** By the United States in Congress Assembled Nov. 1, 1783. Resolution of Congress respecting States unrepresented. Folio.

517 **Broadside.** By the United States in Congress assembled, April 30, 1784, Resolution of Congress in regards to commerce with foreign powers. Signed by Chas. Thomson. (Autograph). Folio.

518 **Broadside.** A note of Shipping-men and provisions sent, and provided for Virginia, by the Rgt. Honorable Henry, Earle of South-hampton, and the company, and other private adventurers, in the yeere 1621. Folio. 4 pages, uncut. Rare.

519 **Broadside.** Supplement to the Alexandria Gazette, Vindicating Judge Bushrod Washington for selling his slaves. Folio.

520 **Colonial Currency.** 5 pieces.

521 **Early American Map.** Nova Anglia Novum Belgium et Virginia. Folio. [1630].

Autographs.

522 **Clarkson, J. L.** Penna. Revolutionary Officer, Letter Signed, Treasury office, July 16, 1781. Folio.

523 **McHenry, Col. Jas.** Aid to Washington. Letter Signed, June 20, 1796, 7 pages. Folio.
   Long and interesting letter, as Secretary of War, relating to the Indians in Tennessee

524 **Brattle, Wm.** Member of the Stamp Act Congress, Loyalist in the Revolution, Benefactor of Harvard College ; Autograph Letter Signed. Boston, 1767. Folio.

525 **Clymer, George.** Document Signed, ½ page, 4to. John Hancock Document Signed. 8vo. Boston, 1765. Benjamin Franklin. "F & D" to Arthur Lee. 8vo. 3 pieces.

526 Calhoun, Jas., and Samuel Smith, Colonels in the Revolution. Autograph letters, signed and addressed, of each, 1782 and 1826. 4to, 2 pieces.

527 Buchanan, Walter. Revolutionary officer of Pennsylvania. Autograph letter, signed, Hanover, March 2, 1778. Folio. To Elias Boudinot.

Interesting letter on the exchange of a prisoner.

528 Franklin, Benjamin. Autograph Document. Folio. 2 pages.

Memorandum of Books sent to the Library May 24, 1755. Receipted by Robt. Greenway, Librarian of the Philadelphia Library.

529 Franklin, Benjamin. Autograph letter, signed, Philadelphia, Sept. 1, 1752. 8vo.

530 Thornton, Matthew, Signer of the Declaration of Independence. Printed Deed, with Blanks filled in by Thornton, March 14, 1770. Folio.

The name occurs twice in the body of the Document.

531 Trumbull, Joseph, Aide to Washington. Autograph letter, signed, Cambridge, May 2, 1775. 4to, 2 pages.

Regarding Tents and Powder for the Connecticut Soldiers.

532 Wilson, James, Signer of the Declaration. Document, signed, March 14, 1791. Folio, 7 pages.

Deposition in regard to counterfeiters of the currency. Sworn before James Wilson.

533 Lafayette, Marquis de, General in the Revolutionary Army. Signed with initials. 4to.

534 Hooper, Robt. L. Revolutionary Officer of Penn. Autograph Letter, signed, Easton, August 27, 1777. 4to.

535 Haskell, E. Revolutionary Officer of Penna. Jan. 14, 1782. 4to.

536 **Walcott, Erastus.** Letter Signed, New London, June 16, 1773. Signed also by Gen. Saml. H. Parsons, Joseph Trumbull, and Nathaniel Wales. 4to, 2 pages.

<small>To John Hancock, asking that any letters received from England, written by persons in Connecticut, inimical to the Colonies, be sent to them, that they may deal with the Authors.</small>

537 **Sullivan, John.** Major-General in the Revolution, Autograph Letter, signed, Durham, 1784. Folio. 3 pages.

<small>As President of the New Hampshire Society of the Cincinnati.</small>

538 **Hazen, Moses.** General in the Revolutionary War. Autograph Letter, signed, New York, March 25, 1784. 4to.

539 **Houston, Saml.** President of Texas. Autograph Letters, signed, House of Representatives, Jan. 12, 1824. 4to. 2 pages.

540 **Nelson, Lord.** Document Signed, on Board of the "Victory" at sea. 5th May, 1804. Folio.

541 **Fulton, Robert.** Inventor of the Steamboat. Autograph Letter, signed New York, June 18, 1814. 4to. 2 pages.

542 **Wolcott, Oliver.** Secretary of the Treasury. Letter signed, June 1, 1795. 4to.

543 **Mercer, Hugh.** Foster child of the U. S. Army. Adopted by Congress. Autograph Letter, Signed. Fredericksburg, July 18, 1825. 4to.

544 **Byfield, Col. Nathaniel.** Judge of the Admiralty for New England. Document signed, 1705. Folio.

<small>Commission appointing John Leverett, President of Harvard College, as his Deputy for Massachusetts Bay, New Hampshire, etc., with Seal.</small>

545 **Queen Anne.** Document signed. Windsor Castle, Oct. 29, 1709. Folio. Signed also by Charles, Earl of Sunderland. 2 pages.

<small>To Lieut.-Governor Jos Dudley of New Hampshire, notifying him, that with this letter, he "will receive a Seal prepared for the use of our Government of New Hampshire.</small>

546 **Grant, Gen'l U. S.** Document signed. Washington, April 21, 1870. 4to, vellum.

547 **Loudan, Lord.** Governor of Virginia. Letter signed. New York, Sept. 7, 1757. Folio. 2 pages.

   In reference to the Winter Campaign of 1757 in New York after the surrender of Fort William Henry, and calling on Governor Benning Wentworth for Troops.

548 **Jackson, Andrew.** Autograph Letter, Signed. March 28, 1829. 8vo.

549 **L'Ouverture, Toussaint.** Negro Patriot. Autograph Letter, Signed. 1797. 4to. 2 pages.

550 **Relic of Slavery.** Pair of Iron Shackles for the Ankle, connected with a chain, used in the Slave Market of Richmond. Neatly mounted in oak case.

551 **Philadelphia Inquirer.** 1861 to 1866, in numbers, 6 vols. Folio.

   Wanting several numbers in 1861, 1864, 1865 and 1866.

PRICES AND NAMES OF PURCHASERS

✣ ✣ SALE OF ✣ ✣

WASHINGTON LETTERS

AND

RELICS

DECEMBER 15 & 16, 1891.

THOS. BIRCH'S SONS, Auctioneers,
PHILADELPHIA.

STAN. V. HENKELS, AUCTIONEER.

LIST OF PRICES AND NAMES OF PURCHASERS.

#	Name	Price	#	Name	Price	#	Name	Price
1	Sabin	$110 00	53	Sabin	$1 80	105	Bradley	$11 00
2	"	87 50	54	Kane	1 20	106	Honeyman	3 50
3	Benjamin, W E	1 00	55	Johann	1 10	107	Sabin	4 50
4	" "	50	56	Benjamin, W R	10	108	Cadwalader	1 00
5	Sabin	400 00	57	Benjamin, W E	60	109	Brock	3 75
6	Kane	6 00	58	Griffin	1 60	110	Benjamin, W R	60
7	Mitchell	5 00	59	Cadwalader	1 25	111	Johann	10 50
8	"	4 00	60	Griffin	1 95	112	Mitchell	15 00
9	Kane	13 00	61	Cadwalader	22 50	113	Benjamin, W E	5 00
10	Sabin	12 00	62	Sabin	1 00	114	Mitchell	2 00
11	Mitchell	3 00	63	Thomas	25	115	"	9 00
12	Benjamin, W R	1 00	64	Bradley	5 00	116	Benjamin, W R	220 00
13	" "	2 75	65	"	3 00	117	Kane	130 00
14	Kane	14 00	66	"	1 00	118	Benjamin, W R	125 00
15	Sabin	1 50	67	"	50	119	" "	105 00
16	Cadwalader	5 00	68	Mitchell	11 00	120	Mount	80 00
17	Benjamin, W R	1 25	69	Benjamin, W R	10	121	Benjamin, W R	105 00
18	Benjamin, W E	3 75	70	" "	10	122	Mount	54 00
19	Benjamin, W R	1 25	71	Bradley	2 50	123	Benjamin, W R	51 00
20	" "	2 25	72	Thomas	20	124	Harrison	655 00
21	Mitchell	2 75	73	Sabin	6 75	125	Morristown	56 00
22	"	8 00	74	Bradley	8 50	126	Benjamin, W R	150 00
23	Benjamin, W R	9 00	75	Mitchell	1 50	127	" "	53 00
24	Sabin	6 00	76	Chapman	2 00	128	" "	135 00
25	"	46 00	77	Cadwalader	1 40	129	" "	85 00
26	Benjamin, W E	4 50	78	Bradley	4 80	130	Kane	115 00
27	Mitchell	4 00	79	Mitchell	20 50	131	Brock, C	160 00
28	Honeyman	6 90	80	Honeyman	7 00	131½	Mitchell	455 00
29	Benjamin, W R	1 40	81	Benjamin, W R	90	132	Benjamin, W E	145 00
30	" "	10	82	Sabin	1 00	133	Benjamin, W R	8 00
31	" "	20	83	Benjamin, W R	40	134	Mount	350 00
32	" "	88	84	" "	05	135	Sabin	31 00
33	" "	55	85	" "	40	136	Mount	70 00
34	Brock	70	86	" "	40	137	Johnson	140 00
35	Benjamin, W R	30	87	" "	40	138	Mitchell	55 00
36	" "	25	88	" "	40	139	"	25 00
37	" "	20	89	" "	40	140	"	24 00
38	" "	10	90	" "	40	141	"	30 00
39	" "	35	91	" "	40	142	"	17 00
40	" "	05	92	" "	40	143	Benjamin, W E	92 50
41	" "	05	93	Mitchell	3 50	144	" "	90 00
42	" "	15	94	Dreer	2 00	145	Mount	100 00
43	" "	05	95	Benjamin, W R	3 50	146	"	100 00
44	Sabin	60	96	Benjamin W E	2 00	147	Benjamin, W E	31 00
45	"	2 00	97	Mount	85 00	147½	" "	13 00
46	Benjamin, W R	05	98	Bradley	36 00	148	Mount	32 50
47	" "	05	99	Sabin	5 00	148½	Benjamin, W R	15 00
48	" "	45	100	"	2 75	149	Mount	90 00
49	" "	05	101	Harrison	3 25	150	Johnson	14 00
50	" "	05	102	"	7 50	151	Chapman	37 00
51	" "	25	103	"	1 25	152	Benjamin, W E	370 00
52	" "	1 00	104	Mitchell	15 00	153	Benjamin, W R	45 00

No.	Name	Amount	No.	Name	Amount	No.	Name	Amount
154	Benjamin, W R	$45 00	203	Mitchell	$1 00	261	Brock	$0 50
155	Dr. Koecker	6 00	204	Sabin	50	262	Sabin	6 00
156	Kay	3 00	205	Marshall	50	263	"	1 50
157	"	2 50	206	Nelson	2 00	264	"	17 00
158	"	1 40	207	Cadwalader	3 00	265	Brock	50
159	"	2 10	208	"	60	266	Sterling	1 50
159A	Kay		209	Mitchell	25	267	Brock	40
159B	"	5 20	210	Marshall	50	268	Judge	24 00
159C	"		211	Mitchell	10	269	Sterling	40
159D	"	1 40	212	"	4 00	270	Brock	60
160	Benjamin, W E	15 50	213	Benjamin, W R	06	271	Sabin	14 50
161	" "	40 00	214	" "	06	272	Bradley	16 00
162	Cadwalader	65 00	215	" "	10	273	Judge	2 75
162½	Benjamin, W E		216	" "	30	274	Sterling	3 00
		240 00	217	Sabin	3 00	275	Geiger	9 00
162¾	Brock, C	70 00	218	Benjamin, W R	1 75	276	Bradley	8 50
162⅞	Johnson	600 00	219	Sabin	11 00	277	Geiger	4 50
163	Benjamin, W R	1 75	220	Sterling	80	278	Brown	6 00
164	Montgomery	3 50	221	Brock, C	50	280	Geiger	10 00
165	Benjamin, W E	4 50	222	Mitchell	1 75	281	Thompson	7 00
166	Benjamin, W R	2 00	223	Benjamin, W E	1 00	282	Sterling	6 00
167	Mitchell	3 75	224	Sabin	1 00	283	Judge	6 00
168	Honeyman	1 25	225	Bradley	1 50	284	Bradley	15 00
169	Benjamin, W E	1 00	226	Brock, C	1 00	285	Judge	4 50
170	Johnson	2 00	227	" "	50	286	Thompson	4 00
171	Brock, C	1 50	228	Mitchell	80	287	Sterling	3 00
172	Cadwalader	50	229	Brock	1 00	288	Thompson	2 75
173	Bradley	1 25	230	Sabin	8 50	289	Sterling	4 25
174	Benjamin, W R	25	231	Brock	1 00	290	Thompson	3 75
175	Brock, C	2 50	231½	Benjamin, W R	1 10	291	Townsend	7 00
176	Mitchell	3 50	232	" "	1 50	292	Sterling	8 00
177	Benjamin, W R	50	233	Bradley	4 25	293	"	10 00
178	Benjamin, W E	1 50	234	Benjamin, W R	50	294	"	15 00
179	Townsend	1 10	235	Mitchell	3 75	295	"	10 00
180	Chapman	2 25	236	Brock, C	3 50	296	Townsend	8 50
181	Brock, C	50	237	Deitz	500 00	297	Hart	2 00
182	Nelson	2 25	239	Herring	60 00	298	Lawrence	20
183	Brock, C	25	241	Cadwalader	50 00	299	Judge	50
184	" "	50	242	Mitchell	30 00	300	"	25
185	Honeyman	70	243	"	30 00	301	Sabin	2 25
186	Mitchell	2 25	244	Herring	210 00	302	"	75
187	Benjamin, W R	1 10	245	Chapman	70 00	303	Lawrence	20
188	" "	6 50	246	Sterling	50	304	Judge	3 00
189	" "	2 50	247	Sabin	1 10	305	Lawrence	20
190	Benjamin, W E	90	248	Judge	1 50	306	"	2 00
191	Sabin	6 50	249	Sterling	2 00	307	Sabin	11 50
192	Brock, C	1 00	250	"	2 50	308	Brock	80
193	Townsend	1 60	251	Whitman	25	309	"	30
194	Brock, C	8 00	252	Sabin	3 75	310	Judge	1 00
195	" "	1 50	253	Brock	40	311	Brock	60
196	" "	1 75	254	Sabin	35	312	Benjamin, W E	5 00
197	" "	2 50	255	"	1 60	313	Sabin	2 00
198	" "	1 50	256	Brock	30	314	Brock	60
199	" "	1 50	257	Judge	60	315	"	25
200	Benjamin, W R	1 00	258	Whitman	30	316	"	25
201	Townsend	1 75	259	Brock	80	317	"	40
202	Sterling	60	260	Sterling	2 00	318	Sabin	50

319	Sabin	$0 35	375	Lawrence	$1 00	432 Judge	$0 50
320	Brock	30	376	Brock	2 25	433 Sabin	1 75
321	Sterling	20	377	Sterling	1 75	434 Judge	5 00
322	Howard	5 00	378	Brock	1 30	435 Marshall	6 00
323	Brock	50	379	Roberts	70	436 "	6 00
324	Judge	1 75	380	Sterling	50	437 "	3 50
325	Brock	50	381	Judge	2 75	438 Sterling	1 50
326	"	25	382	Sabin	2 25	439 "	30
327	"	60	383	Judge	2 00	440 Sterling	1 00
328	"	10	384	Sabin	5 50	441 "	40
329	Lawrence	2 00	385	Judge	4 00	442 Sultzberger	3 25
330	Brock	50	386	Benjamin, W E	1 00	443 Judge	6 00
331	"	25	387	Judge	4 50	444 "	3 00
332	"	50	388	"	1 50	445 "	1 00
333	Judge	1 00	389	Harper	1 50	446 Sultzberger	75
334	Sultzberger	1 40	390	Sterling	60	447 Mitchell	90
335	Thompson	22 50	391	Benjamin, W E	1 25	448 "	3 00
335½	Geiger	27 50	392	Wagner	2 00	449 Judge	25
336	Sterling	4 00	393	Judge	1 00	450 "	1 50
337	Thompson	10 00	394	"	2 00	451 Sultzberger	3 75
338	Judge	4 00	395	Benjamin, W E	1 10	452 Judge	50
339	Benjamin, W E	3 00	396	" "	1 00	453 Sultzberger	1 00
340	Geiger	4 00	397	Mitchell	25	454 "	1 00
341	Thompson	5 50	398	"	5 50	455 Mitchell	5 00
342	Sterling	5 50	399	Brock	80	456 "	2 00
343	Judge	7 00	400	"	70	457 "	3 25
344	Thompson	2 75	401	Lawrence	60	458 Sterling	2 00
345	Benjamin, W E	50	402	Judge	1 60	459 Mitchell	4 00
346	Scattergood	15	403	Sterling	25	460 Jackson	10
347	Sabin	4 25	404	Brock	3 75	461 Sterling	50
348	"	2 25	405	"	50	462 Mitchell	15 00
349	Bradley	1 50	406	Ogden	6 00	463 Sabin	24 00
350	Sabin	6 00	407	Brock	50	464 Sterling	1 50
351	Thompson	6 50	408	Lawrence	2 25	465 Judge	50
352	Marshall	2 50	409	Brock	1 00	466 "	3 50
353	Thompson	7 00	410	"	50	467 Roberts	2 50
354	Geiger	5 00	411	Judge	1 00	468 Judge	1 00
355	Thompson	3 50	412	Brock	1 10	469 "	1 00
356	"	6 00	413	"	2 25	470 Bradley	7 00
357	Thomas	75	414	Judge	2 50	471 Cohen	2 00
358	Judge	80	415	Brock	2 00	472 Roberts	70
359	McWade	1 10	416	"	1 75	473 Lawrence	1 40
360	Marshall	1 10	417	"	4 50	474 Roberts	25
361	Geiger	11 00	418	"	10	475 Sterling	90
362	Thompson	7 00	419	Sterling	05	476 Judge	15 00
363	Brock	2 50	420	Sabin	65	477 Benjamin, W R	5 50
364	"	1 00	421	Brock	2 80	478 Kay	1 00
365	Judge	6 00	422	Judge	5 00	479 Judge	1 50
366	"	2 25	423	Mitchell	25 00	480 Marshall	4 50
367	Brock	50	424	Brock	30	481 Roberts	25
368	"	50	425	"	25	482 Kay	2 00
369	Sterling	40	426	"	4 00	483 Judge	3 75
370	Brock	10 80	427	"	2 00	484 Lawrence	70
371	Judge	5 50	428	"	1 25	485 Judge	1 75
372	Sterling	1 75	429	"	8 00	486 Sterling	2 10
373	Brock	1 00	430	"	40	487 Judge	50
374	"	3 00	431	Benjamin, W E	4 25	488 Ogden	50

489	Judge	$3 75	546	Benjamin, W R	$1 75	628	Benjamin, W R	$6 50
490	Judge	60	547	Brock	2 50	629	Sabin	1 50
491	Ogden	60	548	Benjamin, W R	1 50	630	Maris	75
492	Judge	1 00	549	Mitchell	4 00	631	Crawford	2 25
492½	Roberts	20	550	Benjamin, W R	15 50	632	Maris	2 25
493	Judge	2 00	551	Mitchell	6 00	633	"	1 50
494	Sabin	1 00	552	Benjamin, W R	50	634	Crawford	1 00
495	Honeyman	60	553	" "	05	635	Chapman	25
496	Thompson	90	554	" "	25	636	James	30
497	Judge	2 50	555	" "	05	637	Sterling	18 00
498	Sterling	1 25	556-557	" "	05	638	Burt	13 00
499	Mitchell	1 50	558	" "	3 50	639	James	2 25
500	Sterling	50	559-560	Mitchell	40	640	Burt	26 00
501	Thompson	4 00	561	Sterling	50	641	Sabin	3 50
502	Sterling	2 25	562	Benjamin, W R	30	642	Burt	10 00
503	Judge	1 00	563-565	Mitchell	60	643	"	2 75
504	Sabin	6 00	566-571	Chapman	45	644	X. Brock	5 00
505	Mitchell	3 25	572	Mitchell	45	645	Chapman	41 00
506	Judge	60	573	"	1 75	646	Burt	5 50
507	"	3 00	574	Benjamin, W R	4 90	647	Sterling	3 50
508	Aldrich	58 00	575	" "	80	648	Sabin	51 00
510	Benjamin, W E	3 25	576	Chapman	20	649	Benjamin, W R	7 50
511	Sabin	1 00	577	Benjamin, W R	3 75	650	Sabin	1 00
512	Mitchell	14 00	589	Brock	50	651	Mitchell	60
513	Chapman	25	590	"	50	652	Sabin	50
514	Brock	1 00	591	"	15	653	Mitchell	17 00
515	Benjamin, W E	3 50	592	"	15	654	"	10 00
516	Mitchell	2 25	593	Sterling	15	655	Sabin	6 00
517	"	3 25	594	"	20	656	Chapman	8 50
518	Brock	9 00	595	Honeyman	70	657	Benjamin, W E	2 25
519	Benjamin, W E	1 00	596	Brock	25	658	Chapman	1 50
520	Brock	62	597	Sterling	10	659	"	2 25
521	"	1 00	598	Brock	30	660	Cadwalader	30
522	Sterling	10	599	Lawrence	1 30	661	Brock	80
523	Brock	1 25	600	Brock	25	662	Cadwalader	80
524	Benjamin, W E	50	601	Cash	20	663	Brock	3 50
525	Mitchell	2 10	602	Sterling	10	664	Sterling	75
526	Benjamin, W E	10	603-607	Brock	87	665	Brock	50
527	Benjamin, W R	30	608	"	10	666	Mitchell	3 00
528	Benjamin, W E	3 00	609	"	25	667	Brock	1 40
529	Benjamin, W R	8 00	610	Sterling	10	668	"	60
530	Mitchell	1 00	611	"	10	669	"	30
531	Benjamin, W R	3 25	612	"	10	670	Sterling	1 50
532	Thompson	3 00	613-614	Lawrence	30	671	Brock	60
533	Mitchell	1 75	615	Honeyman	2 25	672	Mitchell	1 00
534	Brock	30	616	Maris	1 50	673	Brock	1 10
535	"	10	617	"	1 50	674	Sterling	60
536	Benjamin, W R	8 00	618	"	1 25	675	Sabin	50
537	Mitchell	5 00	619	"	1 75	676	Roberts	10
538	"	3 00	620	Lawrence	2 25	677	Brock	60
539	Brock	40	621	Benjamin, W R	2 75	678	Chapman	2 25
540	Nelson	6 50	622	Cadwalader	2 25	679	Sabin	50
541	Mitchell	6 00	623	Maris	1 00	680	Benjamin, W R	3 00
542	"	10	624	Sabin	1 50	681	Dreer	16 00
543	Chapman	10	625	Honeyman	2 25	682	Mitchell	1 00
544	Brock	50	626	Sabin	1 50	683	Brock	50
545	Mitchell	10 00	627	Maris	1 50	684	Cash	10

685	Dreer	$9 00	728	Mitchell	$1 00	774 Sabin	$2 00
686	Benjamin, W E	6 50	729	Brock	1 50	775 Sterling	50
687	Francis	25	730	Marshall	50 00	776 Parker	20
687½	Honeyman	30	731	Burt	50 00	777 Jackson	05
688	Campbell	1 25	732	George	240 00	778 Parker	1 00
689	Sterling	80	733	"	140 00	779 Griffin	15
690	Roberts	40	734	Brock	2 75	780 James	20
691	Sterling	80	735	"	6 25	781 Aldrich	70
692	Sabin	3 00	736	Steigerwalt	4 50	782 783 Griffin	60
693	Benjamin, W E	5 25	737	Pine Street	210 00	784 Bradley	27 00
694	Sterling	30	738	"	105 00	785 Cadwalader	50
695	Benjamin, W E	2 00	739	George	150 00	786 Findlay	7 00
696	Sabin	1 00	740	Cotton	180 00	787-790 Brock	1 75
697	Mitchell	1 50	741	George	37 50	791 Campbell	1 30
698	Sterling	90	742	Benjamin, W R	1 35	792 Sabin	15 00
699	Cadwalader	60	743	Brock	2 80	793 Mitchell	62 00
699½	"	1 25	744	Mitchell	1 60	794 Marshall	20 00
700	"	1 00	745	Brock	40 00	795 Mitchell	17 00
701	Sterling	1 75	746	Pine Street	170 00	796 Sabin	21 00
702	Brock	50	747	Cotton	55 00	797 Marshall	5 00
703	Roberts	2 75	748	Benjamin, W E	110 00	798 "	2 25
704	Cadwalader	3 75	749	Brock	9 00	799 Honeyman	80
705	Sabin	1 50	750	"	2 50	800 Mitchell	5 00
706	Sterling	60	751	Pine Street	230 00	801-803 Custer	90
707	Cash	35	752	Nelson	34 10	804 Mitchell	25
708	Sterling	2 20	753	Griffin	20	805 Parker	3 00
709	Aldrich	18 00	754	James	70	806 Brock	5 00
709½	Chapman	12 00	755	Brock	90	807 Parker	1 60
710	Benjamin, W R	325 00	756	James	70	808 Steigerwalt	30
711	Chapman	25 00	757	Mitchell	3 25	809 Brock	1 00
712	Chapman	6 00	758	Griffin	30	810 Mitchell	1 00
713	Mitchell	8 00	759	Mitchell	155 00	811 Chapman	2 00
714	"	9 00	760	Brock	1 00	812 Parker	25
715	"	3 50	761	"	1 50	813 Chapman	1 00
716	Chapman	2 25	762	Brock	25	814 Honeyman	6 48
717	Benjamin, W E	2 25	763	Custer	50	815 Brock	8 00
718	Benjamin, W R	3 50	764	Brock	6 00	816 Griffin	60
719	Brock	3 50	765	"	7 00	817 Bourquin	10 00
720	Benjamin, W E	70	766	Chapman	60	818 McWade	50
721	Crawford	3 00	767	Griffin	50	819 Chapman	10
722	Mitchell	19 00	768	Bradley	2 75	820 Sabin	25
723	"	35 00	769	"	2 25	821 Brock	1 10
724	"	25 00	770	"	5 75	822 Steigerwalt	4 00
725	"	25 00	771	"	2 50	823 Mitchell	3 00
726	Simms	10 00	772	Sabin	3 50		
727	Parker	12 00	773	Brock	4 50		

www.ingramcontent.com/pod-product-compliance
Lightning Source LLC
Chambersburg PA
CBHW022134160426
43197CB00009B/1273